Postmodern Brecht

A Re-Presentation

ELIZABETH WRIGHT

R
ROUTLEDGE
London and New York

For Edmond

First published in 1989 by
Routledge
11 New Fetter Lane, London EC4P 4EE
29 West 35th Street, New York NY 10001

© *1989 Elizabeth Wright*

Printed in Great Britain by
Mackays of Chatham Ltd, Kent

British Library Cataloguing in Publication Data
Wright, Elizabeth, 1926–
  Postmodern Brecht: a re-presentation. ———
  (Critics of the twentieth century).
  1. Drama in German. Brecht, Bertolt, 1898–1956
  I. Title. II. Series
  832'.912

Library of Congress Cataloging in Publication Data
Wright, Elizabeth, 1926–
  Postmodern Brecht: a representation / Elizabeth Wright.
    p. cm. – (Critics of the twentieth century; v. 7)
  Bibliography: p.
  Includes index.
  1. Brecht, Bertolt, 1898–1956 – Criticism and interpretation.
2. Postmodernism. I. Title. II. Series.
PT2603.R397Z9825   1988
832'.912--dc19   88-18696   CIP

ISBN 0-415-02329-7
ISBN 0-415-02330-0 Pbk

Contents

Contents

Editor's foreword

The twentieth century has produced a remarkable number of gifted and innovative literary critics. Indeed it could be argued that some of the finest literary minds of the age have turned to criticism as the medium best adapted to their complex and speculative range of interests. This has sometimes given rise to regret among those who insist on a clear demarcation between 'creative' (primary) writing on the one hand, and 'critical' (secondary) texts on the other. Yet this distinction is far from self-evident. It is coming under strain at the moment as novelists and poets grow increasingly aware of the conventions that govern their writing and the challenge of consciously exploiting and subverting those conventions. And the critics for their part – some of them at least – are beginning to question their traditional role as humble servants of the literary text with no further claim upon the reader's interest or attention. Quite simply, there are texts of literary criticism and theory that, for various reasons – stylistic complexity, historical influence, range of intellectual command – cannot be counted a mere appendage to those other 'primary' texts.

Of course, there is a logical puzzle here, since (it will be argued) 'literary criticism' would never have come into being, and could hardly exist as such, were it not for the body of creative writings that provide its *raison d'être*. But this is not quite the kind of knock-down argument that it might appear at first glance. For one thing, it conflates some very different orders of priority, assuming that literature always comes first (in the sense that Greek tragedy had to exist before Aristotle could formulate its rules), so that literary texts are for that very reason possessed of superior value. And this argument would seem to find commonsense support in the difficulty of thinking what 'literary criticism' could *be* if it seriously renounced all sense of the distinction between literary and critical texts. Would it not then find itself in the unfortunate position of a discipline that had willed its own demise by declaring its subject non-existent?

But these objections would only hit their mark if there were indeed a special kind of writing called 'literature' whose difference from other kinds of writing was enough to put criticism firmly in its place. Otherwise there is nothing in the least self-defeating or paradoxical about a discourse, nominally that of literary criticism, that accrues such interest on its own account as to force some fairly drastic rethinking of its proper powers and limits. The act of crossing over from commentary to literature – or of simply denying the difference between them – becomes quite explicit in the writing of a critic like Geoffrey Hartman. But the signs are already there in such classics as William Empson's *Seven Types of Ambiguity* (1928), a text whose transformative influence on our habits of reading must surely be ranked with the great creative moments of literary modernism. Only on the most dogmatic view of the difference between 'literature' and 'criticism' could a work like *Seven Types* be counted generically an inferior, sub-literary species of production. And the same can be said for many of the critics whose writings and influence this series sets out to explore.

Some, like Empson, are conspicuous individuals who belong to no particular school or large movement. Others, like the Russian Formalists, were part of a communal enterprise and are therefore best understood as representative figures in a complex and evolving dialogue. Then again there are cases of collective identity (like the so-called 'Yale deconstructors') where a mythical group image is invented for largely polemical purposes. (The volumes in this series on de Man, Hartman, and Bloom should help to dispel the idea that 'Yale deconstruction' is anything more than a handy device for collapsing differences and avoiding serious debate.) So there is no question of a series format or house-style that would seek to reduce these differences to a blandly homogeneous treatment. One consequence of recent critical theory is the realization that literary texts have no self-sufficient or autonomous meaning, no existence apart from their after-life of changing interpretations and values. And the same applies to those *critical* texts whose meaning and significance are subject to constant shifts and realignments of interest. This is not to say that trends in criticism are just a matter of intellectual fashion or the merry-go-round of rising and falling reputations. But it is important to grasp how complex are the forces – the conjunctions of historical and cultural motive – that affect the first reception and the subsequent fortunes of a critical text. This point has been raised into a systematic programme by critics like Hans-Robert Jauss, practitioners of so-called 'reception theory' as a form of historical hermeneutics. The volumes in this series will therefore be concerned not only to expound what is of lasting significance but also to set these critics in the context of present-day argument and debate. In some cases (as with Walter Benjamin) this debate takes the form of a struggle for interpretative power among disciplines with sharply opposed ideological viewpoints. Such controversies cannot simply be ignored in the interests of achieving a clear and balanced account. They point to unresolved tensions and problems which are there in the critic's work as well as in the rival appropriative readings. In the end there is no way of drawing a neat methodological line between 'intrinsic' questions (what the critic really thought) and those other, supposedly 'extrinsic' concerns that have to do with influence and reception history.

The volumes will vary accordingly in their focus and range of coverage. They will also reflect the ways in which a speculative approach to questions of literary theory has proved to have striking consequences for the human sciences at large. This breaking-down of disciplinary bounds is among the most signifi-cant developments in recent critical thinking. As philosophers and historians, among others, come to recognize the rhetorical complex-ity of the texts they deal with, so literary theory takes on a new dimension of interest and relevance. It is scarcely appropriate to think of writers like Derrida or de Man as literary critics in any conventional sense of the term. For one thing, they are as much concerned with 'philosophical' as with 'literary' texts, and have indeed – both of them – actively sought to subvert (or deconstruct) such tidy distinctions. A principal object in planning this series was to take full stock of these shifts in the wider intellectual terrain (including the frequent boundary disputes) brought about by critical theory. And, of course, such changes are by no means confined to literary studies, philosophy and the so-called 'sciences of man'. It is equally the case in (say) nuclear physics and molecular biology that advances in the one field have decisive implications for the other, so that specialized research often tends (paradoxically) to break down existing divisions of knowledge.

Such work is typically many years ahead of the academic disciplines and teaching institutions that have obvious reasons of their own for preserving the intellectual *status quo*. One important aspect of modern critical theory is the challenge it presents to these traditional ideas. And lest it be thought that this is merely a one-sided takeover bid by the literary critics, the series will include a number of volumes by authors in those other disciplines, including, for instance, a study of Roland Barthes by an American analytical philosopher.

We shall not, however, cleave to theory as a matter of polemical or principled stance. The series will extend to figures like F. R. Leavis, whose widespread influence went along with an express aversion to literary theory; scholars like Erich Auerbach in the mainstream European tradition; and others who resist assimilation to any clear-cut line of descent. There will also be authoritative volumes on critics such as Northrop Frye and Lionel Trilling, figures who, for various reasons, occupy an ambivalent or essentially contested place in modern critical tradition. Above all the series will strive to resist that current polarization of attitudes that sees no common ground of interest between 'literary criticism' and 'critical theory'.

CHRISTOPHER NORRIS

Acknowledgements

I should like to thank the following for their critical comments on parts of the book: Marilyn Butler, Jochen Fried, Ann Jefferson, and Ian McLeod. My editor Christopher Norris gave unstinting support and encouragement at all stages. My thanks also go to Mieke Bal, Sander Gilman, and Susan Suleiman, and their respective universities Rochester, Cornell, and Harvard for inviting me to lecture and discuss my work in the spring of 1987, just when I needed inspiration. I would also like to thank Ulrich Sonnemann and Christoph Tholen and other members of the Research Centre for Psychoanalysis and Literature of the University of Kassel for the opportunity to lecture and discuss my work on Brecht in the autumn of 1986. As usual, my greatest debt is to Edmond Wright for his constant availability for discussion and help in clarifying the more difficult critical issues.

The staff of the Taylor Institution and Modern Faculty Library in Oxford have as always given me every assistance. Girton College and Trinity College kindly granted me leave in 1986–7 in order to finish the book.

I am grateful to Suhrkamp Verlag for permission to quote from Brecht's works in German. I should also like to thank Methuen for permission to quote from Brecht in translation (*Collected Plays*, translated by John Willett and Ralph Manheim; *Brecht on Theatre* and *The Messingkauf Dialogues*, translated by John Willett), and for permission to translate certain passages myself (those not ascribed in the notes to Willett or Willett and Manheim; these, my own translations, are Copyright © Stephan S. Brecht, 1988).

E.E.W.
Girton College, Cambridge

Introduction

What does Brecht's name mean? He is the German writer and producer who developed a theory of drama grounded in a Marxist aesthetic and thereby revolutionized the modern theatre, even if not society. But this impressive-sounding achievement has in fact incurred wrath and disapproval from each of two opposing camps, that of the East and that of the West. They disapproved because his work disturbed any kind of rigid polarization. Yet it is becoming plain that much of what he proposed and carried out qualifies him to be regarded as a deconstructionist *avant la lettre*.

To put it in terms of the postmodernist debate, Brecht was sceptical of what Jean-François Lyotard called the great narrative, the great danger, the great hero, the great wrong, the great goal, yet he still believed in the possibility of producing by means of his art a form of knowledge that was publicly shareable, a pleasure and a communal tool for understanding. Such a feat of collective labour, involving material produced by author, actor, and spectator, would combine the desire for knowledge with a readiness to help others. This is in contrast to others who, like Michel Foucault, see knowledge arising as a result of a devious opposition to power, as a by-product of oppression. There is, however, a problem, in that for Brecht the new 'scientific' (experimental) knowledge he hopes to gain from his practice in the theatre takes over some of the utopian function of humanist art the facile optimism of which he so firmly jettisons.

In common with the poststructuralist writer/critic, Brecht proclaims that the author is not the creator of an original work, but someone who produces from the materials of history. Brecht is the producer of experimental 'texts' both as regards the writing and the staging of them. He radically opposes any means of

1

representation which make-believes that history cannot be altered. His epic theatre is designed to provoke the realization in the spectator that intervention is a real possibility, and to that end both actors and spectators are invited, even incited, to play their part in the construction of a narrative other than the one that the received version of history proposes.

At a moment when the poststructuralist critic is busy trying to unveil the *latent* production of a bourgeois ideology in literary and critical texts it might be interesting to look at the work of a writer who specially constructs texts in which this same ideology is shown as *manifesting* itself, whose project is to stage an unveiling, to fictionalize this manifesting of a latent content. In terms of poststructuralist theory the famous estrangement effect (*Verfremdungseffekt*), the gestic style, the appeal to the spectator, may be seen as symbolic devices designed to disrupt the imaginary unity between producer and text, actor and role, and spectator and stage, an enterprise which is similar in spirit to Barthes's project in *S/Z* (1975) and *A Lover's Discourse* (1978); in the latter text the titles and marginal notes have an effect he describes as 'à la Brecht' (1978, p. 5), encouraging an estrangement effect at the same time as an identification. For Brecht reality is to be seen as produced by men and women and as transformable by them. The world is not fixed and given. Even contradictions do not exist at the level of the real: only human beings produce them. Whether Brecht's theory and practice is intent on showing that these contradictions can be abolished, or whether he merely suggests that the labour of men and women should be directed towards resolving them is an open question, one which may be followed up in the attempt to unveil the unveiler. As the Series editor's foreword stresses we can no longer rely on a 'clear demarcation between "creative" (primary) writing on the one hand, and "critical" (secondary) texts on the other' (p. vii). The act of 'crossing over' (p. viii) from one to the other is perhaps nowhere more explicit than in the work of Brecht, whose greatest significance for us today, I will argue, lies in his many theoretical works and fragments, as well as in the theory that we can extrapolate from his often contradictory 'pieces' (*Stücke*), as he calls his plays, which have the fruitful habit of continuing to spawn further contradictions. It is not my brief to write a study which deals with the historical Brecht by looking at the influence upon him of movements, such as expressionism and surrealism; the tracing of influences is not relevant to this kind of reading for it precludes

2

being historical about the text itself. It is surely more Brechtian to look for a new historical context for the old theories.

Poststructuralist theory has it that literary texts are a source of knowledge beyond that which they themselves can consciously achieve. Any contradictions revealed by their mode of mediating reality have to be wrested from them. Since Brecht's theory of the text includes dismantling its own ideology, clearly revealing both its mode of production and the ideological positions of the characters, what work is there left for the critic who sees her active role in sitting at her desk changing the world by changing the text rather than by being out in the street?

This book tries to deal with this question via a route which takes in the various views of Brecht on both sides of the Channel, and which allows an examination of the contradictory critical responses (Chapter 1). After a detailed discussion of the 'classical' Brecht's principal theories and concepts (Chapter 2), there will be an attempt to account for the ambivalence of the critical response to his work by an analysis of its comic elements in the light of Freudian and Lacanian theory, leading to a deconstruction of the comedy/tragedy distinction (Chapter 3). Arising out of this attempt, there will be a reassessment of the political and aesthetic solutions he proposes, via a route that goes from a modernist Brecht situated within the context of the theorists of his time (Chapter 4) to a postmodernist Brecht situated within the context of the postmodern stage (Chapters 5 and 6). In conclusion I hope to offer some thoughts on what I see not only as a postmodern reading of Brecht but also a Brechtian reading of postmodernism.

For the convenience of English readers I have quoted Brecht in translation throughout. I have felt it necessary in most cases to supply the original text in the footnotes.[1] This is because Brecht has made a singular contribution to the German literary language. As Heiner Müller (1986, pp. 141–2) points out, the use of the standard language, what we might call the Queen's English and the Germans call *Hochsprache*, always rules out certain grammatical and syntactical choices: Brecht was and still is so important because he de-literalized the language of the stage, drawing upon the dialects of his own region in order to create a new language of the theatre that was neither purely regional nor purely classical. That is to say, Brecht was able to advance with *parole* and at the same time make an impact on *langue*.

3

1 References to the standard translations, where used, are included in the footnotes. The translations from other authors are my own.

1

Misunderstanding Brecht: the critical scene

Brecht's work, owing to its range of theory and practice, is read, performed, and taught, perhaps more than the work of other writers of his stature, via the mediations of past scholars and critics who have become established as an orthodoxy within what might be called a broad church. Thus most informed theatre-goers probably believe that they have a fair idea of Brecht's principal innovations in the theatre and will be able to cite the central categories of his theatrical practice. It seems inevitable that for the moment there is no way of re-reading Brecht without also re-reading the story of his reception.[1] To think through the readings of other scholars has become quite as important as to sort through the formidable quantity of writing that Brecht has left. I would therefore like to give a critical overview of Brecht criticism within the context of my own project, that of co-opting him as post-modernist. If modernism is to be characterized as breaking with tradition while still retaining an individualist stance, then post-modernism can be seen as calling into question both tradition and individualism. In order to indicate something of the way this might be done my account will focus on the issues involved, both explicitly and implicitly, rather than on the precise contributions of the various scholars I draw on. I regard the mediation of recent German scholarship as particularly important for Brecht studies in English, for while German scholars seem to take cognizance of what is being done in English, unfortunately this does not operate the other way round, English scholars rarely engaging with the works of German scholars, except to draw them in as support.

What is the present status of Brecht as a political writer? In the German Democratic Republic (GDR) Brecht has been demoted from national author and is now seen as a big disappointment. In

5

the Federal Republic of Germany (FRG) he is viewed as a pedagogue of the theatre, a rationalist thinker presenting a simplified view of reality. A still-prevailing view on both sides of the Channel is to see Brecht as moving through three phases, from an early subjectivist, or anarchist, or nihilist phase in *Baal* (I make the world), to a middle-period rationalist, or behaviourist or mechanistic phase (the world makes me), to a supposed dialectical resolution of the dilemmas of phase one and two in the late plays (dialectic between self and world), presumed to usher in a third and mature phase. In the past this conclusion resulted in his being seen in the West as a great writer despite being a communist, and in the East in his having achieved a proper dialectic despite his beginning with a decadent aesthetic. The English view is by and large still in support of this version, running from Esslin in 1959 to Suvin in 1984 (except for Dickson, 1978, who organizes Brecht's oeuvre by arguing for a consistent anticipation of Utopia through all his works), but there are now signs that German scholarship, for a long time equally committed to its own three-phase version, is challenging this view by interrogating anew both Brecht's work and that of his critics.[2]

Common to the theories of the three phases is the notion of ultimate continuity. What is seen as the turning point in Brecht's development, his encounter with Marxism in the mid-1920s and his subsequent reversal of the first, subjectivist phase into the second, objectivist one, is painlessly assimilated in a crude notion of dialectic. This moment is given a different interpretation by East and West. The West reads the 'conversion' to Marxism as an outcome of Brecht's personal psychology: the anarchist-cum-nihilist creator of *Baal* (regarded generally as in some sense the *alter ego* of the young Brecht) is searching for firm ground and promptly invents the *Lehrstück*, which enables him to substitute a collective authoritarianism for a self-indulgent individualism. In the third and final phase, there is a synthesis of the two positions, resulting in the 'great' plays. This view has become more refined and sophisticated since its inception by Esslin (1959, p. 137) in Suvin's version (1984), although in an afterword to his book, he would like to amend his 1967 view of a 'non-consenting, a consenting and a mature phase', which he now considers 'too neatly Hegelian'. He is far from oblivious of the political implication of the 'Esslinian bisection into immature (read political) and mature (read aesthetic) phases', but holds that the tripartite scheme 'is probably still of some introductory value' and that 'no acceptable

6

alternative is yet to be seen' (Suvin, 1984, pp. 268–9). What is not immediately obvious is that this tripartite scheme is illicitly shifting an account of biographical stages onto an interpretation of the texts. It is a kind of genetic fallacy, for there is no necessity that an interpretation should be bound to a particular source of influence at a particular time. The ideology of the works is more likely to reveal itself if one attends to their textual elements without recourse to the immediate circumstances of composition.

But even from the biographical point of view the tripartite scheme is not secure. Reiner Steinweg's (1972a) methodical analysis of Brecht's *theory* of the *Lehrstück* as distinct from the content of the plays themselves, together with his presentation of hitherto unpublished material from the Brecht archives, has necessitated a new look at the way Brecht conceived the relation of aesthetics and politics, and this has offered a way out of the three-phase syndrome, since the documents Steinweg has published show that for Brecht the *Lehrstück* was to be the theatre of the future, but there is little sign that it is being taken account of in Brecht studies here (I shall come back to this whole issue, including the problem of translating the term *Lehrstück*).

The German reception

No reader ever reads from a position of neutrality: the reader reacts politically, even and especially where he or she inveighs against the politicizing of the arts. The German reception has its own peculiar fascination owing to its divided interests, that of East and West. A comprehensive article by Michael Schneider (1979) sets out in some detail how Brecht's fortunes have always fluctuated with the political consciousness of the Germans, serving as a kind of barometer of the current climate. During the Cold War of the 1950s Brecht's anti-fascist and anti-militarist plays furnished ideological ammunition against the FRG's policy of economic and military recovery, and during this time Brecht achieved the status of a new socialist classic in the GDR. In the FRG on the other hand, the workers and the petit-bourgeois became wholly preoccupied with the economic miracle (one might instance the reactions of the characters in Edgar Reiz's recent epic film *Heimat*), and evinced no further interest in politics. Hence Brecht's reinstatement as a classic was left to the intellectuals, who were inclined, as in England, to accept the artist despite the Marxist. Brecht's hour as a political writer in the GDR came in the wake of the student uprisings of 1968, when he was hailed by German youth as the communist poet of the day and as the poetic repre- sentative of class conflict, and when, according to Schneider, he became the property of radicals and socialist intellectuals, traded in for the existentialist theatre of Anouilh, Sartre, Camus, Ionesco, and Beckett, with the result that 'the Brecht-boycott of the fifties made way for a regular Brecht-boom' (Schneider, 1979, p. 27). His canonization in the FRG duly followed and he became a classic with an extending influence on the new left poets.

Yet all was not won: his fortunes declined in the early 1970s together with the impetus of the student revolt, at which time he lost his immediate political relevance. He was now set aside to make way for a new cult of inwardness, among whose represen- tatives were Hermann Hesse and Peter Handke, a cult which constituted 'a neo-existentialist revulsion against politics, science, enlightenment', and culminated in 'Brecht-allergy', not to say 'Brecht-antipathy' (Schneider, 1979, p. 29). Yet all was not lost, because before the end of the 1970s this syndrome too became a new commodity, marketed as 'Brecht-fatigue' (*Brecht-Müdigkeit*) (Mittenzwei, 1977, p. 100). At a colloquium held in Frankfurt in 1978 Brecht was deemed inadequate by theatre directors because he could not provide them with enough subject-matter in his plays for their own subjectivity. But this, as will be seen, is really partly a problem of copyright (see 'Wer hat das Recht am Brecht'[3]), namely the extent to which Brecht's plays might be freely used as 'material', as he himself would have approved.

The English reception

Whereas recent German scholars have approached Brecht via the changing relations of aesthetics and politics within a specific historical context (Giese, 1974; Claas, 1977; Voigts, 1977), English scholars have continued to turn out either studies of the man and his work (Dickson, 1978 – though this breaks bounds because it treats Brecht as first and last a political writer), or of Brecht and the theatre (from Willett, 1959, to Needle and Thomson, 1981, to Fuegi, 1987). The introduction of the most recent collection on Brecht and the theatre declares that it 'is addressed to students and teachers of drama and non-academic readers, as well as to the German specialist', the focus being 'primarily on Brecht's place in the German theatrical tradition' (Bartram and Waine, 1982, p. ix). It is still assumed that the history of the modern theatre, culminating predictably in an institutionalized epic theatre with V-effect, will go down well all round, particularly if it includes a 'factual' account of the politico-historical context.

Another tendency of English Brecht reception is to introduce an *ad hominem* assessment on the basis of the contradictions between his life and his art, as in a review by Timothy Garton Ash, which asserts correctly that Brecht was a 'great exploiter: plundering books, friends and women' and was finally 'enthroned in East Berlin, with a West German publisher, Austrian passport and Swiss bank account' (*Times Literary Supplement*, 9 December 1983, p. 1363). Of course the review ends with an all too predictable sentiment: 'The poet Brecht is superbly subversive of every orthodoxy – including his own', or, as Esslin put it in 1959, 'a truly creative writer will have to break out of the narrow limits of the creed to which he has committed himself, namely, by following his own intuition' (p. 208). While Brecht's undoubted opportunism, his autocratic ways with women, and his political ambivalence are of considerable biographical and ideological interest and may make him in some respects an unadmirable figure, they are surely not factors to be held indiscriminately against him when a critical survey of his achievements as a writer is being conducted. Thus it is disconcerting that the most recent account of Brecht's theatrical practice, while being quite illuminating, keeps pointing up the gap between Brecht's socialist views and his privileged position in society, telling us, for instance, that 'Brecht moved in an atmosphere of radical bohemianism while retaining as his home base the comfortable attic apartment with maid service at his bourgeois parents' home and secretarial service at his father's office' (Fuegi, 1987, p. 9). A more objective account of Brecht's *Realpolitik* in the context of his personal and political aspirations and the various circumstances under which he came to live can be found in an article by Pachter (1980). The most systematic answer to the attacks on Brecht's political integrity is given by Brooker (1988), who argues in a close biographical and historical account that Brecht remained as interventionist in his later years as he had been earlier.[4]

In order to understand the English Brecht reception properly, it needs situating in its literary-historical context. Literature's claim to a special place in society has been upheld ever since Sidney's *Apology for Poetry*, which restored to poets their place in the state, denied to them by Plato. In more modern times the advent of Russian Formalism in the 1930s added theoretical weight to the study of literature as an autonomous and specific discipline. Indeed the Formalists' concept of defamiliarization is often loosely taken to be analogous with the Brechtian notion of *Verfremdung*, a point I will come back to. At the same time, and quite independently, Anglo-American criticism came up with a theory which focused on the literary text as such, to be distinguished from all other kinds of writing and to be treated as an object free from everything but literary history itself. A crucial factor was the logical positivist distinction between the language of poetry, regarded as 'emotive', and the language of science, regarded as 'referential'. Brecht's 'theatre of the scientific age' (*GW* 16, pp. 700–1) strives precisely to do away with this alienating division of science and art, even though he himself necessarily works with a historically bound positivistic view of science.

The English Brecht reception may therefore be seen as rooted in the Anglo-American tradition of literary studies, untroubled by any notion of 'reception theory', to the extent that English critics rarely tangle with other critics the way that German critics do.[5] The overwhelming feeling here is that it is both more instructive and more pleasurable to go back to the supposedly immutable and unchanging primary text or to the account of actual productions rather than to confront critically the work done by others in the field. Other critics, if used at all, are mainly in the footnotes, to give credibility to scholarship, or, if in the running text, they are respectfully acknowledged. At most, they may be used for some point of disagreement in interpretation, while any genuine controversial material, the result of the *position* from which the criticism is launched, is largely ignored.[6] The interpretative enterprise of most English criticism goes counter to Steinweg's work on the *Lehrstück* without any sign that it has taken his point. But until Brecht's *Lehrstücke* are considered as a central theoretical contribution in his work and not merely restricted to their content, scholarship is not likely to get beyond the three-phase reading of Brecht in some form or other (for a full discussion – in English, though not published in England – of the *Lehrstück* in the context of a radical break with tradition, see Kamath, 1983).

Is Brecht dead?

It is clear from the foregoing that Brecht is far from dead as an object of critical interpretation, but the question remains whether he is dead as regards making a live contribution to the theory and practice of the theatre. And here there is no consensus. Werner Mittenzwei defines his term 'Brecht-fatigue' as a symptom of the 'aesthetic emancipation of socialist literature' (1977, pp. 101–14). The aesthetic deposing of Brecht by his former pupils (he cites Peter Hacks in particular) may be seen as a reaction against Brecht's asserted positivistic belief in reason and science and against his 'aesthetic of contradictions'. Mittenzwei argues that in a socialist society it is no longer of grave import to confront an audience with the contradictions of reality; instead it is the subjective factor which will once more engage the interest of those who have achieved socialism. There is room for a new attitude with a consequent gain for aesthetic 'playfulness'; art and science may again be seen as distinct realms, whereas Brecht had brought them together. Brecht's successors argue that a new society has need of a new aesthetic: why bother to show in art what can now be learnt from reading Marx and Lenin (Mittenzwei, 1977, p. 107)? Aesthetic emancipation means that art is no longer required as a means of changing society, and therefore is not called upon to produce a direct social effect.

However, neither for Mittenzwei nor for the authors in question does this herald a return to the old bourgeois reception with its notion of catharsis as a release of pent-up emotion. Mittenzwei argues the need for another kind of catharsis which takes account of those contradictions that are not as easily assigned to class conflict as Brecht had supposed. The problem is, however, that upholders of the dialectic in the GDR are bound to find themselves in a dilemma, in that they want to hold on to the dialectic while maintaining that a synthesis has been achieved (the problem of the contradictory reality of socialism is central to the works of Heiner Müller, as Chapter 6 of this book shows). The most recent debates in both East and West have been in the theatre world and suggest that there is a strong feeling that Brecht cannot be merely reproduced *à la lettre*, that to use his work uncritically is a betrayal (Müller, 1980). A new volume of essays analyses the symptoms of 'Brecht-fatigue' with a view to re-discovering the actuality of Brecht's praxis (*Aktualisierung Brechts*, Haug *et al.*, 1980). To investigate the most recent area of debate I now need to make a short excursus into the issue of the *Lehrstück*.

The *Lehrstücke* are a particularly sensitive point in the reception of Brecht both as a theoretician and a practitioner of the theatre, the problem surfacing in the very attempt to translate the term. The choice, itself of ideological significance, has in the past been

11

between 'didactic plays' (Esslin, 1959), 'propagandist plays' (Gray, 1976), and 'learning plays' (Speirs, 1982). Of these, 'learning plays' is clearly the term most appropriate in the light that Steinweg's research casts on Brecht's radical notion of a theatre for the future, but more recently the term 'teaching plays' has been suggested as suitable for plays that are 'not merely plays that teach, but also plays about teaching' (Nägele, 1987, p. 115). However, since the German term *Lehrstück* combines the crucial combination of teaching and learning, I prefer to retain it.

The *Lehrstücke* are a group of nine plays written around 1929 to 1930 and designated as such by Brecht to distinguish them from other plays written in the same period, the most frequently discussed being *The Measures Taken* (*Die Massnahme*, 1930).[7] Critical reception on both sides of the Channel and on both sides of the Wall has generally regarded them as purveyors of Marxist doctrine, though there is considerable disagreement regarding the success of this imputed intention. The plays coincide roughly with the beginning of Brecht's study of the writings of Marx and are seen by East and West alike as the turning point in his supposed tripartite development. As products of his 'vulgar Marxist' phase these plays are regarded by the East as failing in aesthetic quality on account of the rigid form and by the West as failing in literary complexity on account of their rigid content. These failings are considered to be surmounted when their author achieves, according to the East, a mature political consciousness or, according to the West, a personal psychological maturity.

These tidy views were challenged by the appearance of Reiner Steinweg's book *Das Lehrstück* in 1972, which followed on from the researches he published in the journal *alternative* the previous year. Steinweg makes available the new, previously unpublished material, which he relates to Brecht's various pronouncements on the subject.[8] From this fresh perspective he analyses and evaluates the *Lehrstück* as a model for the theatre that must be sharply distinguished from the epic theatre. According to Brecht's own directives (*GW* 17, p. 1024), this type of theatre is for the benefit of the actors and requires no audience, but this has been misunderstood and misrepresented, for the actors are conceived not as professionals, but as amateurs: school students, worker collectives, and groups of all kinds. Crucial among the material that Steinweg recovered from the Brecht archives is a fragment which briefly distinguishes between 'Major Pedagogy' and 'Minor Pedagogy' (*Grosse Pedagogik* and *Kleine Pedagogik*) (Steinweg, 1972a, p. 23).

These are two strategic programmes in miniature, pertaining specifically to the *Lehrtheater* (learning/teaching-play theatre) as distinct from the epic theatre. It is the function of Minor Pedagogy to cater for the transitional period and subversively to undermine bourgeois ideology without breaking too radically with bourgeois traditions; hence the categories of actor and spectator may be retained while the bourgeois spectator is being encouraged to raise his consciousness. Major Pedagogy, on the other hand, presupposes the existence of a socialist state and is thus a *model* for a radically different theatre of the future, where the distinction between actor and spectator is entirely wiped out. The actors, all amateurs of one kind or another, occupy a double role of observing ('spectating') and acting, working and re-working a communal set text which is perpetually alterable, the object being to turn art into a social practice, an experiment in socially productive behaviour. Unlike epic theatre, which exposes the contradictions while perpetuating the institution which produces them, *Lehrtheater* breaks with the bourgeois theatre and provides a new revolutionary praxis. It offers a trial text, not only in the sense that it is often organized round the thematics of a trial, but also in that it allows the text to be tried out in practice and changed by those who are undergoing the learning experience. To discuss Brecht's *Lehrstücke* purely from the point of view of their content or even their form, without considering and testing out their function, is completely to miss the point. However, this is not to deny the difficulty of according the status of a new aesthetic to the *Lehrtheater*, while in the case of the epic theatre it had been relatively easy.

Although Steinweg's breakthrough, as already mentioned, has hardly caused a tremor in the ranks of English scholarship, in Germany it has at least provoked a certain amount of critical reaction. Predictably the opposition falls once again into two camps, though both are united in denying that the new theatre has a general validity as a radical new aesthetic: the West maintains that the plays are bound to a particular historical moment, when Brecht was intent on creating a productive audience (Berenberg-Gossler, Müller, and Stosch, 1974), while the East declares that this was the beginning of a new materialist aesthetic, to be superseded by the superior aesthetic of the epic theatre (Mittenzwei, 1977, pp. 718–21).

The poststructuralist reception

There is yet a further reception, namely that by the theorists of theory, the critical theorists of the poststructuralist era. This reception amounts to the production of a Lacanian Brecht by two modern critical theorists, each of whom uses the theories of the French psychoanalyst and thinker Jacques Lacan: Rainer Nägele (1987) draws implicitly on Lacan to elaborate Brecht's *Lehrstück* in the context of a radical theory of the modern theatre; Stephen Heath (1974) draws explicitly on Lacan in order to work out Brecht's contribution to a new theory of the cinema.

To Steinweg must be given the credit of rescuing the *Lehrstück* from its premature classification as either an exercise in rigid Marxist ideology or as an example of unintended humanist tragedy. But in arguing that the point of the *Lehrstück* was and is to provide a practice-ground for the revolutionizing of social and political relations and for ultimately getting rid of the theatre as a bourgeois institution, he relied entirely on the letter of Brecht's writings, this being the point of his archival researches. The result was an over-concentration on a hitherto neglected element, the formal aspects of the plays: the staged confrontations, the rehearsals of antithetical positions, and the way Brecht had conceived of an enactment of the dialectic via an exchange of roles among the actors.

For Marx, of course, the dialectic is primarily a historical process, its dynamic being the contradictions that arise out of the structuring of economic systems, which lead to their inevitable re-ordering and replacement. Although he and Engels acknowledged dialectic as turning up in problems of logic and language, they tended to place these as a form of further proof of the universality of the dialectic. However, the dialectic is more directly attributable to the nature of human communication than they were able to acknowledge: the dialectic is the pattern of the change of any concept or meaning that results from the source of reference being placed in a new context of relevance, a new intentional perspective. It does not necessarily follow, then, that the dialectic is progressive.

Against Steinweg's view there has recently appeared a current of opposition, which can itself be seen as a dialectical movement, for, in arguing against Steinweg's harmonizing formalism, the new position has taken in something from the old *Lehrstück* critique. In a recent collection of articles on the use of the *Lehrstück* for lay-actors (Steinweg (ed.), 1978), Hans-Thies Lehmann and Helmuth Lethen argue that the focus on form reduces the dialectical element of the plays to such a degree that there is nothing left of dialectic. From the very beginning there is an assumption that a resolution must be striven for – the Young Comrade in *The Measures Taken* has already been killed when the play begins and the solution of the agitators is tested out for truth or falsity after the event.

A brief outline of the issues raised in the play might help to clarify the argument surrounding the *Lehrstücke*. The action takes place in pre-revolutionary China. Four communist agitators, represented by one woman and three men, are being judged by their party, backed by a control chorus. They have been engaged in communist activities, in the course of which they were forced to shoot their youngest comrade. In order to show the court of law the necessity of the measure they have taken the four agitators repeat the situation and show how the Young Comrade has behaved in a variety of situations. The protagonists who evolve out of the chorus are both actors and spectators of the action. The Young Comrade is a part that is demonstrated, each of the four agitators being given a chance to take this part and test it out. The Young Comrade never has any personal identity; he is a mediated figure, existing by virtue of the collective. Since the four agitators consist of one woman and three men, he might sometimes be a she. The actors demonstrate that although the Young Comrade had the commitment of a revolutionary, he was not able to exert sufficient discipline over himself and did not listen to the voice of reason. He inadvertently became a great danger to the movement, for he gave himself away by showing pity for the plight of a coolie who was one of a team labouring to pull a rice boat up the river: the Young Comrade wants to serve the revolution but cannot bear that the individual should suffer in the meantime. But what is expected of him is that he should identify with the plight of the coolies as an oppressed class and not with that of the single coolie. The aim of the revolution is to change the conditions: the play shows that human beings have only commodity value, that the few are exploiting the many, that the many are working for the few. When the many recognize this state of affairs, they will develop a new consciousness, the consciousness of a slave, as Hegel defined it, who sees that his labour is essential to the existence of the master. Although the Young Comrade believes this he is unable to act on it. Hence he consents to his own execution.

Humanist and Marxist critics have seen the play as an indict-ment of the party's machiavellianism: the humanists thought that Brecht was being Leninist and the Marxists feared that the play would be seen as Leninist by the humanists. Neither made any allowance for the possibility of a tragic ambiguity which might vary according to historical circumstances. But Lehmann and Lethen maintain that a second level of dialectic is implied in the content of the plays which transcends a first level of opposition, that of individual versus collective, spontaneous action versus rational assessment. The second level reveals that there is no such simple opposition, for the body's needs and responses are not precisely definable and hence rationality can only operate on a level of hypothesis in assuming that it has named everything that goes on within a body. Nor can there be a purely spontaneous act, since human action cannot exist without some kind of symbolic understanding. This puts paid to any notion of a dialectic of given oppositions, for what emerges from the interaction of bodies and societies cannot be so crudely separated. Bourgeois criticism, then, was not so far off the mark in pointing to tragedy, though this is not to herald a return to a humanist tragedy with its image of a consoling order beyond the grave. The frame of reference is no longer the same, for, as Nägele observes, there is 'a small and yet radical difference between that which cannot be integrated after working through the dialectic of things and the sentimental contra-dictions before that work has taken place' (Nägele, 1987, p. 115).

The strong reaction against the *Lehrstück* suggests a powerful subjective content, something left over, not solved. This something has left traces of violence and terror, the effects of which critics like Steinweg have disregarded. Even though past critics have misread these effects, they were at least not immune to them, whereas now they tend to get tidied away. In the past the com-munist side regarded the plays as either good theory, acting out the methods of dialectic that are characteristic of human interac-tion, or bad theory, showing a defective dialectic, a mechanistic set of antitheses which would only serve to give communism a bad name. The bourgeois side ignored theory and focused on content, perceiving terror either as the effacement of the individual in keeping with communist doctrine, just what the communists had feared, or as the tragedy of the individual, overwhelmed by inevitable circumstances. The bourgeois reading thus emphasized tragic conflict, untroubled either by Steinweg's research or by theory. Lehmann and Lethen argue for a different tragic element,

16

a remainder which cannot be encompassed by rationality, that escapes the dialectic, that testifies to the pain of unresolved contradictions.

The body is ultimately outside the collective's definition; the body is never a given self. Subjecthood, the foundation of the body, is here sharply distinguished from selfhood: it is the collective which grants the subject its status as a self but it does not provide that from which the self is made. The tragic moment is therefore far from being purely existential, since the existential is political through and through. The political strategies and decisions of the learning plays are to do with fitting subjects into theories, with finding a theory which includes and accounts for the needs of bodies.

This new approach to the *Lehrstück* thus rejects a false dialectic based on simplistic oppositions such as reason versus emotion. Indeed it reveals that the forming of collective images can be a violent process. Hence Nägele (1987) argues against the way the theatre of Brecht is generally contrasted with the theatre of Artaud, the former characterized as rational, ascetic, and distanced, the latter as irrational, emotional, and violent. Nägele regards such a polarization of concepts as a symptom of a repetition compulsion on the part of reason to work with the given oppositions of the mystical-irrational versus the political-rational. Dramatists such as Peter Weiss, Heiner Müller, and Edward Bond, who combine Brecht and Artaud, have taken their cue from that critical potential within the works of Brecht and Artaud which challenges those very polarizations. Nägele argues that these works subvert any simple opposition by showing that the biological body is not identical with the body image as granted to the subject by society: Brecht's theatre reveals the discordance in the body, because by means of his *gestus* he shows that the body's gestures always include its relation to other bodies; like Artaud's theatre Brecht dwells on the violence done to the body by the inscription of Law. In neither case may the body present itself as complete in itself, but what identity it has comes from the system which has given it its place in a code of social relations. As will be seen (in Chapter 6 of this book), it is this aspect of the *Lehrstück* which critically engages Heiner Müller.

The *Lehrstücke*, then, do not mark a transitional phase between early and late Brecht, nor do they neatly fit into Brecht's theory, as reconstituted by Steinweg: a harmonization under the banner of a great pedagogy for the future. According to Nägele, Steinweg's attempts to work with Brecht's theory of the *Lehrstück* in practice make these plays seem more in keeping with Habermas's model of the Ideal Speech Situation (1970), than with Brecht's conflictual texts (Nägele, 1987, p. 115). Although Brecht likes to promote the idea that learning is imbued with the pleasure of experiment, in the *Lehrstücke* this pleasure is bound up with the shock of violence. The plays deal with antagonisms which exceed the given oppositions. They reveal the contradictions that any prevailing order wants to suppress, such as that help and violence go together: in the 'clown scene' of the *Baden Learning-Play on Consent* (*Das Badener Lehrstück vom Einverständnis*, 1929) two small clowns 'help' a large clown by sawing him apart. This is far from returning to the old bourgeois oppositions, which were taken to pre-exist any dialectic (for a further discussion of this play, see Chapter 3, p. 59–6).

The work of estrangement is as much a critique of reason as an attempt to install it, and the audience is to engage in this work together with the text and the production. With the *Lehrstück* the actor-cum-spectator has to learn a form of multiple identification, splitting him-/herself into multiple identities reaching across a variety of parts and positions, recognizing each time the mismatch of body and social role, analysing the strong emotional effect, be it pleasure or pain, as the price of being inserted into a collective, a Symbolic Order of language and law. Take the example of *The Exception and the Rule* (*Die Ausnahme und die Regel*, 1929–30), where the Coolie makes a gesture which, from his view of the collective, is an offer of help, even though his offer is motivated by self-interest. In the Merchant's context of interpretation, that of mistreating the Coolie, it can only be a threat to his life. In law the Merchant's interpretation is deemed the proper one, and he is exonerated from his killing of the Coolie. The rule was unable to recognize the socially valuable act, an analogy of the body being misinterpreted by society, an ambiguity not perceived. The rule did not yield to the exception. Within the play a dialectical occasion is ignored, a lesson that goes beyond the particular society in which it occurs. The actors-cum-spectators learn the cost of political repression (for a further discussion of this play see p. 64–5).

It is in this sense of being a school of dialectics that the *Lehrstück* has been taken up as a model for a social and political practice by theorists of the cinema such as Stephen Heath. Where the *Lehrstück* provides an art for producers rather than consumers, the cinema, Heath argues, has no such model. It is primarily the art of the product, the spectator being cut off from production and performance. Though Brecht himself has contributed to a revolutionary cinematic practice with his film *Kuhle Wampe*, a film conceived, written, and produced by a collective, with specific techniques and strategies to engage the spectator actively, it is not so much any direct relevance this may have which interests the theorist of the cinema. Rather, Heath points out, Brecht has raised questions about the cinema which have a wider relevance, particularly as regards the kind of intervention artistic practices might make. These practices are to be seen as part of a general struggle in ideology against the representations it produces, encouraging that process Brecht designated as 'interventionist thinking' (*eingreifendes Denken*). A Brechtian practice in the cinema will be in direct opposition to the founding ideology of the cinema, that of giving the spectator the illusion of an all-perceiving eye, thereby installing, as in Lacan's mirror-phase, an Imaginary ego. The aim is rather to show the positions of both subject and object within a process of production.

This is where the concept of *Verfremdung* comes in for the theorist of the cinema, as 'distanciation', for other translations make it all too easy to fall into the temptation of treating this effect as a mere artistic device. ('Estrangement' is also an acceptable translation, avoiding the socio-economic implications of 'alienation', but I prefer to avoid the translation of specialist terms; I am using the compromise term 'V-effect' wherever possible.) For Heath and other recent theorists (for example, Knopf, 1974) *Verfremdung* is a mode of critical seeing that goes on within a process by which man identifies his objects. It goes beyond the concept 'defamiliarization': it sets up a series of social, political, and ideological interruptions that remind us that representations are not given but produced. Contrary to popular belief, *Verfremdung* does not do away with identification but examines it critically, using the technique of montage which shows that no representation is fixed and final. The V-effect may be directed at ideology in general, including that of Marxism, so it is no argument to regard it as a stylistic peculiarity of Brecht's of which he already availed himself in his pre-Marxist days. It is political through and through, for it shows that the spectator is never only at the receiving end of a representation, but is included in it. In Lacanian terms the V-effect disturbs the Imaginary mirror-relation of the spectator with his/her own image, upsetting the complacency with which the current self-image is being viewed. The V-effect introduces a Symbolic dimension by being an investigation of what Lacan calls the Symbolic Order, forcing the spectator to relate him- or herself to a pre-existent social order by examining his or her representations as tied to a mode of production. The spectator is theatricalized in Brecht's theory, made to realize the fictional elements in his or her own existence. Brecht's theory and practice of intervention, as Heath calls it, is directed at the ideology of representation and the way this assigns subjects pre-determined positions (one thinks of *Man is Man* in particular; see Chapter 2, pp. 33–6).

For Brecht the *gestus* reveals how relations of production determine our social relations where we believe them to be at their most 'natural'. Art can only make its representations from within ideology (from within a subject's unconscious determinations), not from some pure spot outside it. The *gestus* is the exaggerated ideological gesture, for one might say that every gesture is a *gestus*, just as, re-reading Freud through Lacan, one can say that every word is a Freudian slip. Even brushing away a fly, which Brecht produces as an example of a gesture free from social import (*GW* 15, p. 483), is not without its cultural aspects.

The link between Nägele's and Heath's reading of Brecht is that they each implicitly reveal the V-effect as dialectical in its very form. It operates by provision of dramatic clues on stage and screen which ambiguate the supposedly natural illusion. The ideology of the theatre and cinema is shown to be attributable to the ideology of the world, more specifically the bourgeois world. As with a jester who produces a rival clue to another context of desire to disrupt authority's interpretation, so the V-effect is produced by a similar succession of rival clues. The division in the spectator's subjectivity is foregrounded, reaching through to the desires of that body that inhabits the existing forms and awakens it to an understanding of its own socialization and the discovery of its political repression.

To continue to stage Brecht relying on the well-known and well-loved devices, the haunting tunes and witty turns, is to end up with museum pieces, rather than radical theatre. A recent production at the Royal Shakespeare Company of *Mother Courage* (*Mutter Courage*, 1949) with Judi Dench in the title role made this all too plain. The only striking V-effect was that the audience had to wait some thirty minutes because a fault in the electrical equipment put the mechanics of Mutter Courage's wagon out of action. When the stage curtain finally rose on the bare stage there were embarrassed apologies to the effect that the wagon would unfortunately have to be pushed. What is more, it was pushed not by people who were obviously stage hands, but by hooded figures, looking more like sinister monks than workers, darting about with silent stealth, hiding behind the wagon as much as possible. The effect was unintentionally ludicrous and typified the failure of the performance to call upon the audience to be productive in any way. It might be compared with another production, that of the Boston Shakespeare Theater Company (*Boston Review*, Suleiman, 1984). This production seems to have been more in keeping with the postmodernist Brecht I have been sketching out, for it aimed at a general theatricalization of the body on the stage with a corresponding effect in the spectator. Gone was any notion that to think and feel simultaneously is somehow against the grain of the theory. There was a strong sense of identification, achieved by a certain stark naturalism in the midst of the bare, non-illusory stage. There could be no doubt that there were real bodies on the stage. The reviewer notes the time it took for Mutter Courage to wrap up her daughter's body, struggling to get all the limbs tucked into the rough shroud, and also the time it took to pluck clean a tangibly real chicken, feather by feather. But the most startling real effect of all took place because the company could not afford a large carved crucifix such as the Berliner Ensemble used on stage, and hence the producer constructed a 'live' crucifix by getting an actor in position, on a wooden cross raised up on a platform, his arms outstretched, head on one side. The actors were thus made to perform real acts in real time, rather as in the Dance Theatre of Pina Bausch (see Chapter 6 in this book). The V-effect of this is stunning, for the combination of bare boards and real bodies makes the spectator acutely aware from the co-presence of illusion and actuality that bodies are bound together by illusory agreements. Aesthetics and politics are here united, for the aesthetic becomes a metaphor for a political condition, forcing the spectator to see that illusion is a part of reality.

Would it not be better to read, teach, and stage Brecht as a source of discontinuous insight, extracting from his theory and practice what seems most valuable at the time, rather than continue to purvey the three-phase package? And would it not also be better not to take his theory as canonical, to abandon that gleeful interpretation, that hoary old chestnut in its many varieties, that Brecht is more Aristotelian than he meant to be? Or, in its modern version, *is* as Aristotelian as he meant to be? Rather interrogate the theory in the practice (like Rainer Nägele) and the practice in the theory (like Stephen Heath), treating both his dramatic and theoretical works as 'experimental pieces' (*Versuche*), investigating the many provocative fragments and essays, and giving the now reified *Short Organum for the Theatre* a rest.[9] To end with a letter purloined from Marx: the critics have merely interpreted Brecht in various ways, the point now is to change him.

Notes

1 This task has been greatly eased by two excellent 'handbooks' by Jan Knopf, which methodically and polemically offer critical inventories to Brecht's theatre (1980) and to his poetry, prose, and socio-political writings (1984). Both are invaluable pedagogical aids.

2 See Knopf (1974) for a rigorous and comprehensively annotated account from a radical perspective, and Mittenzwei (1977), who provides an anthology of critical perspectives by GDR authors dating from 1949 onwards.

3 Becker (1981) discusses the considerable problems of getting permission from Brecht's publishers and heirs in order to stage Brecht in any revisionary form. Theatre companies have to guarantee that their production will be 'faithful to the text' (*werktreu*): 'But with this empirical, non-determinable "rubber-concept" (*Gummibegriff*) Text-Fidelity, the artistic freedom to interpret in the theatre (and the creative staging of a theatrical text) will be restricted in a way that can hardly be calculated in advance' (p. 2). In a similar vein Christy (1986) writes in the *Guardian* about the vicissitudes of a new Brecht translation for a recent production of *The Threepenny Opera*: 'Every line of MacDonald's translation of Brecht's opera for beggars has to be sent to Berlin for vetting by the Brecht estate. When you look at the NT's script you can see which bits have passed the echt Brecht test' (p. 13). But see also Unseld (1980) for an account of the problems arising from the editing and publishing of Brecht's works.

4 Brooker's book *Bertolt Brecht: Dialectics, Poetry, Politics* (1988) can be seen as complementary to mine in that he is reinterpreting the historical documentary evidence about the emergence of Brecht's theories, where I am engaged in a re-interpretation of the theories themselves.

5 In this section I have not dealt with American reception as such. However, current American critics writing on Brecht, such as Rainer Nägele, and other contributors to the journal *New German Critique* are referred to throughout as providing revisions of the English reception. There is, perhaps fortunately, no systematic account of Brecht, no *n*-phase Brecht, emanating from America, that could be challenged. An excellent biographical account of Brecht's fortunes in America has been given by Lyon (1982), which, however, has no immediate bearing on my project.

6 Thus Speirs (1982), who in his book, *Brecht's Early Plays* broaches a promising argument for a correspondence between Brecht's subjectivity and the versions of Marxism he espoused, takes no issue with Steinweg's work, and it is all too clear from his chapter on the *Lehrstücke* that his treatment of them follows the pre-Steinweg reception. Moreover, the opportunity of introducing this work to the 'student reader' (for whom this book is intended, p. 4) is lost again.

7 There are five versions of this play (see Steinweg, 1972b). After its first performance in 1930, which included a brief questionnaire for the audience (*GW* 17, p. 1034), there followed some half dozen further performances, after which the play was forbidden by national-socialist censorship. After the war it suited Brecht not to lift the ban: he did not wish the play to be performed. He is reported to have said to his theatre director, Manfred Wekwerth, that this play was what he envisaged for a theatre of the future (see Chapter 6 of this book for Heiner Müller's play *Mauser* as a critique of *The Measures Taken*).

8 Steinweg (1978) has usefully summarized Brecht's conception of the *Lehrstück* as follows:

  (i) *Lehrstücktheater* is a theatre without audience.
  (ii) The *Lehrstücke* work with negative, that is, asocial models of behaviour, shown via attitudes, modes of speech, and gestures.
  (iii) These plays are not out to show development of character, but work up from a variety of angles contradictory interpretations of situations deriving from a given problem, rather like a musical theme and its variations.
  (iv) They are not to be taken as proving points by means of illustrations in the text.
  (v) The texts are rather to be regarded as experimental models, provoking criticism and adjustment by the players in the course of their stage practice.

9 Richard Baumgart (1987) writes in *Theater Heute*: 'At present Brecht's *Organum* reads as if written by a cheerful monk, an angelic doctor, clever, inoffensive, instructive, mild, breezy and virtuous – a perfect Indian summer' (p. 20).

2

Brecht in theory and practice: refunctioning the theatre

What is the status of Brecht's Marxism and of the theory of the theatre designed to promote it? The aim of the new theory is to show the relations of production within the work that shape it, thus bringing the consumer into close contact with the production process. The author is no longer just a hidden persuader, but openly solicits the collaboration of the spectator. The V-effect is not just an 'aesthetic device', as for the Russian Formalists, for whom such devices opened doors of perception to the possibility of the object. For Brecht it is an instrument for changing reality, not the object; it is a social device, undoing the effects of reality under bourgeois capitalism. The 'object' is already distorted by ideology: what Brecht is after is to provoke the audience to want to change the social reality that goes on producing distorted objects, including persons.

In 1928 Brecht began to study with the revisionist Marxist thinker Karl Korsch (1886–1961), who focused on the subjective and activist aspect of Marxist politics, as distinct from the more orthodox and deterministic doctrine. Brecht referred to him as his 'teacher' (*GW* 20, p. 65), but found him more activist in theory than in practice and expressed some disappointment. It was with him, however, that he first developed a concept of dialectics, not as a universal historical principle, but as a critical method of intervention (Brüggemann, 1973, pp. 88–9). Marxist theory was inherent in Brecht's concept of theatre from the beginning. From 1920 onwards he took a critical stance against traditional theatre and was soon preoccupied with developing two types of theatre, an epic theatre designed to reveal the contradictions in bourgeois society and a *Lehrtheater* which aimed to revolutionize the bourgeois theatre (see Chapter 1). Later he became dissatisfied with the term 'epic theatre' and revised his ground rules in order to accommodate the new designation, 'dialectical theatre'. I shall try to take account of these differences, though not in an over-systematic way, because Brecht's writings resist such an approach.

Brecht's theory is not a closed system, but is scattered about his writings in the form of aphorisms, poetic fragments, working notes, and instructions. Hence it is misleading to take a *Short Organum for the Theatre* (*Kleines Organon für das Theater*, 1948) as mandatory, as chief repository of all cumulative wisdom or lack of wisdom, when what it does is to offer a summary of Brecht's aesthetic of contradictions. It might be taken as an example not so much of the content of the theory but of the fragmented form in which the theory appears. I shall now examine representative examples of Brecht's theory and practice, while at the same time continuing to work out further his key concepts.

Non-Aristotelian theatre

In the texts gathered together under the rubric 'On Non-Aristotelian Drama' (1933–41) Brecht attacks the concept of empathy (*Einfühlung*). According to Aristotle, mimesis, the imitation of an action, is to effect a catharsis whereby the audience is purged via the emotions of pity and fear. Brecht wants to transform 'fear' (*Furcht*) and 'pity' (*Mitleid*) into 'desire for knowledge' (*Wissensbegierde*) and 'readiness to help' (*Hilfsbereitschaft*) (*GW* 15, p. 301). With this new combination he is promoting pleasure in discovery, that is, learning as a project of the Renaissance, but without the bourgeois connotation of excessive striving, as in the later development of the *Faust* theme (see Knopf, 1980, p. 441). Brecht does not want knowledge reduced to the status of a commodity, but would like it to be combined with pleasure in making new discoveries, coupled with displeasure at the present state of affairs. Knowledge is to become praxis, that continual adjustment of meanings which results from the interaction of changing human need with the contingencies of nature. For Brecht knowledge is that which results in a process of continual transformation of the world as we know it. What he calls 'The Gay Criticism' (*GW* 16, p. 637) redirects bourgeois inquisitiveness based on individual self-interest into channels that can serve the interests of a new class:

This critical attitude of the spectator (that is, towards the

25

material, not towards the execution of it) must not be seen simply as a purely rational, calculating, neutral, scientific attitude. It must be an artistic, productive, appreciative attitude. It represents in art humanity's turn to a practical criticism of nature, including humanity's own nature. . . . As I see it, this new, inquisitive, active, inventive attitude is in its significance, scope and pleasurable content in no way inferior to the old Aristotelian catharsis.[1]

Brecht's non-Aristotelian theatre is designed to promote a new attitude, another way of seeing, towards which end he 'refunctions'[2] the whole business of staging (from 1918 onwards Brecht worked with the brilliant painter and stage designer Caspar Neher, an old schoolfriend of his). The stage sets undergo a radical change from looking like traditional ready-made constructions to looking like constructions in progress, which required active interpretation as regards their function (see 'On Designing the Stage Sets of the New Non-Aristotelian Drama', *GW* 15, pp. 439–54). Whatever props are used, they are there not just as realistic background, but as something to be acted upon. Every play required its own special stage set to bring out its particular point. A new type of curtain, which did not close off the stage from the audience, replaced the old heavy one, and thus worked against the traditional notion of the stage as 'fourth wall', beyond which the spectator was permitted to cast a voyeuristic look. Frequently there was no curtain at all; the emphasis in every case was on the relation between stage and audience as joint participants in the production of the text, with the spectator remaining aware of the 'real' world and hence able to judge the text's continuing usefulness in the light of the stage events.

Under the rubric of 'Short Description of a New Technique of Acting which brings forth an Estrangement Effect' (1935–41) Brecht collects together a series of pronouncements to do with the technical aspects of his theatre. These theoretical pronouncements go with the theory of the non-Aristotelian epic theatre and point to the fact that Brecht's theory is not only to do with the art of the actor, but also with the art of the spectator. It cannot be stressed too often that for Brecht the V-effect is not a value-free technical device. He is aware that it was used in other cultures (*GW* 15, p. 362), but insists that he wishes it to be used dialectically, as an expression of a real relation, and that it be aimed at the interests of a particular class for whom it is to promote revolutionary change by pointing to what is historically outmoded:

> The theatre, which in our time became political before our eyes, had not been apolitical up to then. It had taught us to view the world in the way that the ruling classes wanted it to be viewed . . . Now the world could and had to be represented as caught up in development and continuous process, without any limits being laid down by any one class regarding these as necessary to its interests. The passive attitude of the spectator, which essentially corresponded to the passivity of the great majority of people in life, made way for an active one.[3]

The audience is to be nudged into a critical and inquiring attitude by a continual emphasis on the fictional status of the theatrical enterprise. The audience is not allowed to forget that it is sitting in the theatre, yet, at the same time, it must be prevented from bringing along the same set of expectations that it has in life: an active productive state is to replace its passive consumer mood. Hence the first condition of the V-effect is that 'stage and auditorium must be purged of all that is "magical" and that no "hypnotic fields" come about' (*GW* 15, p. 341); the transferential tendencies of the audience must be neutralized via a whole range of artistic devices (see Chapter 3, pp. 55–7). Contrary to popular misconception, this does not mean that the actor needs to give up *all* attempts to get the audience to empathize, but that he does it differently: he does not gain sympathy for himself by provoking a personal act of identification, but gains it for another by demonstrating that person's plight in his relation *to* others: 'A *gestus* shows the relation of people to one another. A work task, for instance, is not a *gestus*, if it does not imply a social relation, such as exploitation or co-operation.'[4]

Every emotion is to be turned outwards and manifest itself as a set of social relations. The empathy that the Brechtian actor solicits will thus not be an end in itself, but a means to an end. The actor will use it as a preliminary (*Vorstadium*) (*GW* 15, p. 342), as a lure to the spectator, somewhat reminiscent of Freud's theory of 'fore-pleasure' in art (Freud, 1908, p. 153), with the difference that the 'release of still greater pleasure to come' is not tied to the business of fulfilling private personal wishes but of engaging in productivity and change in the public domain. Hence Brecht emphasizes that the actor should perform his part as a reader (*Leser*) rather than as a reciter (*Vorleser*), aware of the effects that the text produces on him. He should give the impression that, although he is performing a single action, this implies a choice of a number of alternatives, including the opposite of what he is doing. All action is the result of a choice: there are many alternatives which may be ideologically concealed. Some of these may not even have been considered by the person, but this does not release him from the responsibility of not having chosen them. Brecht thinks it is high time that the audience should take this responsibility upon itself.

So how does he set about his declared aim of engaging the audience's critical interest and how successful is he in his endeavours? In this chapter I want to intersperse appropriate examples of Brecht's practice with discussion of particular aspects of his theory. In discussing his plays I shall concentrate on what he calls *Die Fabel*, a term of art which cannot be adequately translated: it is the moral of the story not in a merely ethical sense, but also in a socio-political one. The *Fabel* (a term I shall retain throughout) does not simply correspond to actual events in the collective life of human beings, but consists of invented happenings. The stage figures are not simple representations of living persons, but invented and shaped in response to ideas. The *Fabel* is the 'core of the theatrical performance', the 'sum total of all the gestic incidents' (*GW* 16, p. 695), and all the various V-effects have to be seen as contained within it, not mechanically listed as mere stage effects. To reveal the *Fabel* is to engage with the discourse of the text.[5]

One of his early attempts to construct an epic theatre was *The Threepenny Opera* (*Die Dreigroschenoper*, 1928). The source of Brecht's piece is John Gay's *The Beggar's Opera* (1728), translated by Elisabeth Hauptmann in 1927–8. But whereas the action in Gay's opera is determined by the individual characters, in Brecht's version it is determined by the prevailing economic circumstances:

> The world is poor but man is bad.
> We should aim high instead of low
> But our condition's such this can't be so.[6]

The economic circumstances are to be revealed and the disguise stripped away:

> See the shark with teeth like razors.
> All can read his open face.
> And Macheath has got a knife, but
> Not in such an obvious place.[7]

Gay's *The Beggar's Opera* takes place at the beginning of the eighteenth century, the century that saw the rise of the bourgeoisie. Brecht's play takes place at a time when the bourgeoisie is well established, but at no specific historical moment. However, it is notable that Brecht presents the kind of bourgeois society which was the forerunner of what was to be characteristic of twentieth-century capitalism.

The theme of the play is the bourgeois as gangster, but also the gangster as bourgeois. The bourgeois order relies and depends on the status quo, where every object, human and non-human alike, is a commodity called by another, more flattering name. The police are seen to protect those who constitute this order rather than those who become the victims of it.

Macheath is an entrepreneur who lives at the expense of his employees, a gang of petty thieves. He enters into business relations with a capitalist called Peachum and into a pseudo-marriage with his daughter Polly. Jenny, a prostitute, for whom he pimps, sells him to the authorities in turn, thereby demonstrating the commodity value of men and women alike. In common with Polly, his pseudo-wife, she regards him as her property; she depends on his regular Thursday afternoon visits to the brothel. Both women see him as their property and both prostitute and bourgeois daughter are for sale: beneath the veil of comic sentiment all the people are shown as effects of the system while at the same time they collude with it.

The beggar likewise becomes a commodity, a victim of society, selling his hideousness as the women sell their attractions. In Brecht's version of the opera the beggars are not even allowed to keep the gifts bestowed on them, but have to hand them over to Peachum in return for a wage. Macheath and Peachum both comically demonstrate the principle of capitalist labour: the degradation of men and women to the status of commodities, while at the same time the demand is made that they hand over the fruits of their alienated labour. Yet finally the old myth comes to the gangster's rescue: a pardon from the king's messenger on horseback. In the end the bourgeois order cannot fail its representatives. This particular V-effect is integral to the *Fabel*.

Marxist critics find the play frivolous, arguing that the farcical elements endear it to a bourgeois audience and thus rob it of any true critical potential. Bourgeois critics praise it for what they regard as a general statement on human nature in its ever-present predatory wolfishness:

What keeps mankind alive? The fact that millions
Are daily tortured, stifled, punished, silenced, oppressed.[8]

Unfortunately for Brecht's intentions, though not perhaps for his box-office success, the alluring lyrics of Kurt Weill had an effect beyond their content; they acted as a narcotic and were received as popular songs. The reviews in Brecht's time reflect the entrenched positions of East and West (as outlined in Chapter 1):

> Of social or political satire there is not a trace . . . all in all, a varied and entertaining mishmash. Bert Brecht, who, not for the first time, successfully makes an attempt at reviving an old piece, cleverly hits the jargon of the gangster- and rogue-milieu. And the audience is greatly taken with it. (*Die Rote Fahne*, 1928; in Wyss, 1977, p. 83)

> [Twenty years ago] one hailed the Mac-the-Knife piece with a flourish of trumpets, today one celebrates it as poetic production (*Dichtung*). Formerly one felt in its aggressiveness the expression of a social condition, today one understands it as theatre, play, fun. (*Münchner Merkur*, 1949; in Wyss, 1977, p. 87)

A recent performance (National Theatre Company, 1986) gained new relevance from the phenomenon of unemployment in that the 'beggars' clearly demonstrated the positions to be adopted in a system where they were expected to behave as if the attitudes to them were charitable. The fight between Jenny the whore and Polly the 'wife' also rose above slapstick, showing not merely two jealous women, but two people caught in rivalry over a bourgeois hero and rendered absurd in their commitment, one poking an umbrella at the would-be pregnant other, the other poisoning the food of her rival, then snatching it away as both become united in sentiment. The overplayed farce pointed to the general purposelessness of these attitudes. But as the earlier reception shows, the epic elements were too easily absorbed into the old theatre. A better model was clearly needed for a more rigorous practice. Even so, the success or failure of the Brechtian theatre can never entirely be a question of the text, unless it be that the audience is included as an effect within it. No playwright-cum-director can work autonomously, as Brecht's *Messingkauf Dialogues* (see below, pp. 38–40) make only too plain.

The epic model

By 'epic', Brecht is broaching a definition which transcends the traditional concept of the genre. The epic (*das Epische*) is not only not tied to a particular genre, but it can also be found in other genres, taking with it its connotations of narrative distance. The drama thereby surrenders the old characteristic quality of suspense, together with its concomitant effect of luring the audience into purely subjective identifications and the final granting of emotional release. Instead the stage begins not only to narrate but also to comment and criticize from a viewpoint not necessarily tied to the immediate action.

The hallmark of the epic theatre is its emphasis on the production of the text. Brecht's aesthetic is based upon a view of the text that has become mandatory in poststructuralist theory: the text as site of production, involving author, reader, and an Other, which for Brecht is history. In order to bring home to the audience the productive potential of the text, Brecht has to create narrative distance by his technique of writing, staging, acting, and directing, as already discussed. The whole of the theatre must change its form, not only the text or the actor or the performance: the audience too must alter its attitude. The constant interruption of the narrative works to create a distance between stage and audience. The analogy of 'all the world's a stage' is stood on its head, because for Brecht this does not imply that the stage is life: rather, the fictionality of life, the re-writability of the text of history, offers a model for the theatre.

Brecht's essay 'The Street Scene' ('Die Strassenszene', 1938) (*GW* 16, pp. 546–58) has occupied a shifting place in his writings (see *GW* 16, notes, p. 5*). Subtitled 'A Basic Model for a Scene of an Epic Theatre', it clearly testifies to Brecht's liking for models which could function as analogies to the models of the empirical sciences, enabling him to demonstrate in a reductive form the ideological function of so-called 'natural' processes. The 'street scene' refers to the 'natural scene' which takes place in the street when there has been an accident, and various victims and witnesses of this accident try to reconstruct for bystanders or police exactly what has happened. The resulting attitudes, demonstrations, arguments are, according to Brecht, analogous to the 'artificial' epic theatre (*GW* 15, p. 557), yet at the same time they show that what he calls 'epic theatre' is not a wilful invention displacing the 'natural' theatre, the point being that there is no such thing. Both epic and 'natural' theatre have demonstrators who show their interests, spectators who are caught up in the events and prepared to take the role of arbitrators. In each case there is an interplay of art and life: the experience is 'repeated' and theatricalized, rather than imitated as if it were happening for the first time.

So how does the analogy work? An eye-witness is performing a dramatized account to a group of bystanders, demonstrating with the help of gestures how, in his view, the accident occurred. Brecht stresses the artificiality of the narrative and the elements of the production process:

> The performance of the street demonstrator has the character of a repetition. The event has happened, what is taking place here is a repetition . . . the rehearsed elements become plainly apparent, namely, the text learnt by heart, the whole apparatus and all the preparation.[9]

The street demonstrator has to show the event with a particular distance; he must not identify with the bearing of the other but must 'quote' him, so the audience will see the split between who speaks and who is spoken: 'He never forgets, nor lets it be forgotten, that he is not the subject, but the demonstrator' (p. 553). This encourages the spectator to identify with the demonstrator rather than with the character he is demonstrating, trying to decide in what way the incident is meaningful: 'The object of the performance is to make it easier to assess the incident' (p. 558). The Brechtian actor, of course, will be biased against the prevailing power structure and will show intentionally what the street demonstrator reveals unintentionally: that the capitalist ideology produces effects both on-stage and off. But the acting of both will be different from that practised in the theatre of illusion, because the gestures of the epic narrator will not be mimetic, but interpretative.

In the 'street scene' the demonstration has the material aim of revealing the circumstances of the accident, in particular, who was responsible among agents and agencies. The outcome may affect the compensation of the victims, with consequences all round: 'The driver risks dismissal, loss of licence, a prison sentence; the victim risks a large hospital bill, loss of job, permanent disfigurement, perhaps unfitness for work' (p. 550).

Both natural street theatre and artistic epic theatre share the fact that the demonstration is done for a social purpose and has social significance. Brecht's theatre is an attempt at a social intervention, whereby the prevailing power structure must be felt to be intolerable and act as a trigger for the critical process of analysis, with both author and spectator equally involved in challenging the text. Like the 'street demonstrator' they will look at 'character' in its social and historical context:

> To the street demonstrator the *character* of the person demonstrated remains a quantity that does not have to be entirely defined. Within certain limits he can be this way or that way, it does not matter. What interests the demonstrator are his accident-prone and accident-proof qualities.[10]

To become more accident-proof is to become aware of what kind of ideology determines one's acts within a social structure. The *gestus* of the narrator will reveal the degree of personal and political repression (for a more extended analysis of this aspect in a different context, see Wright, 1987).

A play which responds well to these epic criteria is *Man is Man* (*Mann ist Mann*, 1926), earlier than *The Threepenny Opera*, and not so easily taken over. With the writing and staging of this play Brecht began to develop a variety of effects to complicate his themes and motifs: songs, inserted texts, self-reference, and the self-presentation of characters. The *Fabel* of this play centres on the transformation of an individual through his insertion into a collective. At the beginning of the play Galy Gay is a porter, at the end he is a soldier. There are two aspects to the theme of this transformation, the loss of individuality which Galy Gay suffers as a sign of the times (the age of mass-production), and the gain of a new identity which he acquires as a member of a collective. There might be two different responses to this dual view: the bourgeois side might see it as a warning against such a transformation, and that is how the play has often been received; the communist side would see it as an affirmation that the individual is defined not in opposition to a collective but through its support. The 'comedy', as Brecht called it, tends to play off one view against the other.

Galy Gay is a porter from old Kilkoa, a seaport in India. When the curtain rises, his wife is peeling potatoes and he is sitting beside her, the picture a *gestus* of petit-bourgeois contentment. He is clearly content with his situation, but to complete his desire he wants to buy a fish at the right price for his income and station. On route to market he comes across three drunken British colonial soldiers, running away after having broken into an Indian temple.

In the course of their escape they abandoned a comrade because he lost a tuft of hair while trying to get away and was thus left with an incriminating bare patch on his head. Galy Gay agrees to take the place of this soldier in a roll call so that the crime will not come to light. He puts on a uniform and takes the new name, Jeraiah Jip, in return for cigars and brandy.

Indeed Galy Gay seems predestined for such a transformation. He is slow – said to run no faster than a goods train – has nothing to lose, and is too poor to afford the luxury of individuality. A place in a collective is thus shown to be a gain for him.

A stock critical response to the play is to see it as representing a socialist art movement called 'New Objectivity', which protested against the objectification of the individual and represented men and women as totally determined by external circumstances. But what Brecht shows is rather that objects, including people, are produced via the relations of production in which they are engaged. This *Grundgestus* (basic gest) is embedded in the play's interlude, entitled 'The Elephant Calf', a farce in which Galy Gay is tricked into selling a pseudo-elephant, played by two soldiers covered over by a huge map. Galy Gay agrees that it must be a real elephant, as soon as a buyer appears on the scene: 'Elephant is elephant, especially when it is for sale' (*GW* 1, p. 343). Galy Gay sells it, whereupon it is immediately exposed as a false buy and used as a threat against him: he is compelled to keep his new identity to avoid the accusation of selling army property under false pretences. What is being demonstrated is not only that a person is as transformable as an object, but that nothing has any value in itself (such as Galy Gay's elephant), apart from the value it acquires when a buyer comes who is prepared to give it a value, thereby turning it into a product.

Galy Gay gains a new personality via production and activity. He is re-assembled just like a motor car (p. 336), and turns into a 'human fighting-machine' (p. 376). By this means Brecht gets rid of the old concept of individuality. In contrast to Galy Gay is the Sergeant ('Bloody Five') who gained his reputation through a criminal act: shooting five soldiers to test out his gun. A bourgeois hiding inside his uniform, he assumes a 'character' he does not possess. His only claim to individuality is his erratic sexuality (it comes on whenever it rains) which he finally sacrifices in an unheroic act of self-castration, so that he may retain his uniform self.

Galy Gay's re-assembly is shown as a farce, yet it is connected with the economic principle of its time. Brecht's play is not an expression of the New Objectivity, but rather a demonstration of its laws: man is nothing without social/economic relations. He becomes an individual only when inserted into them. These relations, however, are not in the first instance human relations, but relations of things and commodities, which also include men and women. Man is made uniform, literally and metaphorically, and hence the army serves as an example; but the army is also a radical mirror-image of bourgeois society (as Brecht shows in *Drums in the Night (Trommeln in der Nacht*, 1919) and also in *Mother Courage*, war is a continuation of bourgeois business). The illusion of the bourgeois individual is thus demystified.

'Once is never' (p. 314): the tendentious theme of the play says that, as in mathematics, it is only the series which assigns meaning. 'One is no one. One has to be addressed by another' (pp. 360 and 362); man only comes into being via the language of a collective, by being called upon to occupy a place. Identity is not there from birth, but produced within a signifying system. Here Galy Gay is re-assembled in the collective as the 'human fighting-machine' (p. 376). In a later preface to the play Brecht writes: 'Galy Gay actually takes no harm, but makes a gain' (*GW* 17, p. 978). Brecht wants to demonstrate that the development of capitalism with its emphasis on the masses here opens a new possibility for determining human identity. As will be seen in Chapter 4, Brecht placed great hope in a culture for the masses. But although he is aware of its negative aspect, he has as yet no idea of fascism and its exploitation of the collective consciousness, which resulted in the abuse of the human fighting-machine. The Lacanian echo of the theme of man as signifier for another is transcended, or sidestepped, whatever the case may be, by Brecht's fierce belief in the historical contingency of any system and his lifelong fight to challenge all fixed orders. For him Marxism was a mode of critical analysis which could be turned on itself: the concept of a transindividual order would have been anathema to him.

Man is Man is a comedy which plays with its material in a variety of ways: the audience is addressed; the action commented upon; figures speak of themselves in the third person; Brecht is cited in the text; there is a large element of clowning which serves as a method of demonstration; Galy Gay himself reflects on his own fortunes. Brecht is the demonstrator, the director of the play within the play, distancing the audience from the happenings on the stage, presenting them with the lesson that reality in the theatre is an analogy to reality in life, since in each case interventions may be made and events can be played and re-played differently.

The reception of this piece was more informed than that accorded to *The Threepenny Opera*. No unqualified approval but a clear understanding of the issues:

> Bert Brecht quite clearly has it in for 'character-nuts' (*Charakterköpfe*) – as his term goes. 'Character-nut' is a disturbance of the normal human type by the personal and individual. 'The greatest joy of humankind' is now no longer the personality – as Goethe would boldly have it. Well, since humankind hardly consists of Goethe and his lot, one cannot altogether disagree with Brecht when he tries to find salvation for good old average humankind in a standardized type. (*Frankfurter Zeitung*, 1926; in Wyss, 1977, pp. 53–4)

Towards a dialectical theatre

The attempt will now be made to get from epic theatre to dialectical theatre. According to our view and intention the praxis of the epic theatre and its whole conception was by no means undialectical, nor can an epic theatre get by without an epic element. Nevertheless we have in mind a considerable transformation.[11]

What, then, is the distinction between epic and dialectic? What does Brecht gain by calling this new set of texts 'Dialectics in the Theatre' (1951–6) (*GW* 16, pp. 869–941)? Brecht felt that the term 'epic' did not adequately define the changing state of things. He wrote a series of appendices for the *Short Organum*, because he thought that 'epic' was too formal a category for the kind of theatre he was trying to achieve, since its apparently clear opposition to 'dramatic' theatre gave rise to misunderstanding. Although epic theatre was the prerequisite for a dialectical theatre it could not of itself set free the productivity and transformability of society, which is where the true sources of pleasure are to be found (*GW* 16, p. 870).

Dialectical theatre goes in for a mode of representation which continually reveals the contradictions in the incidents and objects it singles out:

> This technique allows the theatre to make use in its representations of the new social scientific method known as dialectical

materialism. In order to unearth society's laws of motion this method treats social situations as processes, and traces out all inconsistencies. It regards nothing as existing except in so far as it changes, in other words is in disharmony with itself. This also goes for those human feelings, opinions and attitudes through which at any time the form of men's life together finds its expression.[12]

These contradictions are not fundamentally opposed but denote one and the same thing in its contradictory aspects (Brecht's play *The Good Person of Setzuan* will serve as one such example). The contradictions are within whatever situation is identified: there is no unity or univocal meaning. Contradictions appear as the socio-historical expression of the conditions represented; indeed, they are the very condition of representability. The assumption that there must be unity is based on the vain hope (as that of the ego's in Lacan's mirror phase) that where there is a split there must have been unity. But it is human beings who produce contradictions and hence the world must be subject to criticism and change. The dialectical process points to relations between persons and their contradictory interactions in social life:

> The bourgeois theatre's performances always aim at smoothing over contradictions, at creating false harmony, at idealization. Conditions are reported as if they could not be otherwise. . . . If there is any development it is always steady, never by jerks; the developments always take place within a definite framework which cannot be broken through.[13]

Brecht felt that the epic theatre, by continuing to concentrate on the technical devices made possible by the new technology, did not sufficiently keep in mind the function of these devices: that they were meant to be used to foster critical observation and stimulate activity in the social domain. His *Short Organum for the Theatre* is frequently cited in a programmatic way, as a list of definitions and prescriptions. Brecht put on record his view of it as a summary of *The Messingkauf Dialogues*:

> More or less finished *Short Organum* for the theatre; it is a short summary of the *Messingkauf*. Main proposition: that a certain kind of learning is the most vital pleasure of our age, so much so, that it must play a large role in our theatre. In this way I was able to treat the theatre as an aesthetic enterprise, which made it easier for me to describe the various innovations. Thus

the critical attitude in respect of the social world loses the odium of the nonsensuous, the negative, the inartistic, with which the prevailing aesthetic has saddled it.[14]

The Messingkauf Dialogues (*Der Messingkauf*, 1937–51) is rightly regarded as Brecht's most distinguished achievement, but not often discussed, presumably because of its length (*GW* 16, pp. 499–650). *Messingkauf* in the German title means 'brass sale', a metaphor which depends on a story (told by one speaker to another) concerning an argument over the selling of a trumpet:

> The particularity of my interest so strikes me that I can only compare myself with a man, say, who deals in scrap metal and goes up to a brass band to buy, not a trumpet, let's say, but simply brass. The trumpeter's trumpet is made of brass, as so many ounces of brass. All the same, that's how I ransack your theatre for events between people, such as you do more or less imitate even if your imitations are for a very different purpose than my satisfaction. To put it in a nutshell: I'm looking for a way of getting incidents between people imitated for certain purposes; I've heard that you supply such imitations; and now I hope to find out if they are the kind of imitations I can use.[15]

Here the trumpet stands for the theatre in its old interpretation, and the brass for the theatrical material that is to be refunctioned. The dealer who wants to buy the brass is only interested in the worth of the brass, not the worth of the trumpet; if he is offered the trumpet he will disregard its value as a musical instrument. Similarly, the Philosopher in *The Messingkauf Dialogues* (the teller of the tale) is not interested in the greatness and aura of a particular dramatic art, but only in its possibility as material for a change of function, namely, what the old theatre can contribute to a new one, which he calls 'thaeter' to distinguish it from the old. Further, if the trumpet is 'art' and the brass is 'material', the question is also to what extent the old art did justice to reality. The Philosopher is interested in what is being represented, not in the representation. The value of the representation depends on the degree to which it has managed to capture by every possible means the fluctuating reality of the present.

The argument of *The Messingkauf Dialogues* is shared out between a philosopher, a dramaturge (general stage adviser), an actor, and an actress, who hold meetings to discuss what might be done about a new art of the theatre. This set of texts has not been as controversially received as the *Short Organum*, probably because it is in the form of a dialogue, written to be staged (parts of it were performed by the Berliner Ensemble in 1963). In *The Messingkauf Dialogues* Brecht conducts an ideological critique of the traditional theatre, analysing its social function and its effects. He does not merely examine the aesthetic effect of such a theatre, the restoring of the balance of the emotions, but its political intention and effect (which might be seen as getting rid of rebellious feelings). Brecht proposes that the ritualistic elements of the theatre be played down, allowing the focus to be on experimentation: the theatre is to test out the unspecified laws of society. Art is to play its part in a general transformation of society and cease to be treated as an autonomous realm.

In the course of the dialogues the participants take up certain positions in the debate, though it is the Philosopher who rather wins the day. He represents those who were the first to make scientific discoveries; he is the one who wants to discard the brass trumpet and put the material to new use. He argues for the new theatre, which is to transform society, just as Marx transformed philosophy, namely, not merely by interpreting the world, but by changing it.

The Actor, on the other hand, wants to maintain the present state of affairs, for it is clear that he continues to favour a tragedy of fate. It is the Philosopher's task to reveal the hidden strategies of power implied in this kind of drama and to show how the autonomy of art unwittingly supports and canonizes the institution. He argues that in mimesis, the imitation of an action, what is being ignored are the contradictions in the world; this precludes all possibility of change. He pleads instead for a new concept of realism, in which aesthetic means are used to represent the world as process: the V-effect is to reveal how the laws of society operate, demonstrating that nothing is normal and natural for all time, and thus intervening in the process. The present state of affairs becomes the object of a historical analysis, just as in the 'street scene' (re-integrated into the text of *The Messingkauf Dialogues*) the narrative of the witness is a historical reconstruction of an event that has already happened. A new concept of art emerges, art as a social practice, in which the emotions are given their place and are not opposed to reason. In the end the actors agree that the demand for a scientific probing of reality does not hurt the theatre: as reality changes, so must art, if it is to capture the new reality. What is needed is productivity, fantasy, feeling, and invention.

Various practice scenes are inserted into the dialogues in order to show how the classics might be performed now. For instance, in Schiller's *Maria Stuart* the conflict between the two queens is reduced to a quarrel between two competing fishwives, with the original version performed alongside the revised one.

A review of *The Messingkauf Dialogues* runs as follows:

> A performance by the Berliner Ensemble which combined all things in one: criticism, examples, direction, dramatic art, literary writing. . . . Four persons: philosopher, dramaturge, actor, actress, hold discussions about the theatre, interrupted and supplemented by drama- and film-extracts which serve as examples and counter-examples. . . . The critical discussion on the theatre itself turned into theatre. Points made did not simply remain points, but became dramatic effects, so that criticism revealed pathos, popular jargon, sentimentality, with an immediately clarifying and rational effect. (*Die andere Zeitung*, Hamburg, 1963; in Wyss, 1977, p. 401)

A good example of Brecht's dialectical practice in the theatre is provided by his play *The Good Person of Setzuan* (*Der gute Mensch von Sezuan*, 1941–3). Three gods are sent from heaven to find out if the world is of the kind that will allow a sufficient number of the human race to lead a life worthy of that name. The gods have been listening to complaints about the ways of humankind for two thousand years. But note that the question is not whether human beings are good or bad, but whether the world will do as it is. An experiment is to be carried out, in the course of which the three gods are to observe the ways of the world. The gods appear twice, once at the beginning of the play, when the experiment starts, and once at the end, when they pronounce upon it; in between they only appear in a dream or as observers.

They begin to search in vain to find accommodation for the night, until Shen Te, a prostitute, offers her hospitality. She is specifically asked not to tell anyone in case it brings them into disrepute: the gods are presented as men of the world who are anxious not to lose their reputation. Before leaving they give Shen Te money for their board and lodging, with which she tries to start a business. But she cannot both lead a charitable life and keep her business. In order to carry on in business she invents a cousin, Shui Ta, a 'bad' self, who can say no. The argument of the play is plainly dialectical: human beings can only be good if they are simultaneously bad. Hence the world *must* be changed.

The gods have to abandon some of the conditions of their 'experiment', for in the course of their exhausting search they can only find *one* good human being, Shen Te. They finally make a hasty departure, helplessly opting out of the experiment. Thus the bad world drives the gods away, leaving the human beings to continue the experiment for themselves. The play ends with a dialectical challenge for the audience, who are left to justify the existence of their world to others, instead of justifying the ways of God. Neither theology nor theodicy here offer a way out. Men/women have to justify the ways of men/women to men/women (Shen Te being suitably split by a difference within).

At the beginning of the play, Shen Te, as prostitute, is on the lowest level of the socio-economic order: she sells herself. Love of another is here again reduced to love of another as a commodity. (The play was first conceived (in 1930) as a short sketch entitled *Die Ware Liebe*, *Ware* meaning 'commodity' and *wahre* meaning 'true', hence 'The Commodity/True Love'.) Through the gifts of the gods Shen Te is able to climb up a couple of rungs of the ladder: after buying a tobacco shop she can number herself among the petit-bourgeois, as above the workers. Simultaneously, those who have lost their shop have to go down the ladder; they lose the roof over their heads and join the *Lumpenproletariat* (the deposed bourgeois 'free floating' mass, vulnerable to reactionary ideologies and movements, such as fascism). Shen Te's new position enables her to enter into the laws of capitalist exchange: as a business-woman she can only make a profit if she takes and gives nothing away. Hence there is a need for a 'bad cousin', who takes care of the trade, while she as 'good person' keeps away from the buying and selling. Thus Brecht is able to show the real split of the bourgeois individual into private moral self and public business self. The split person as an embodiment of capitalism has nothing to do with any notions of schizophrenia: s/he is the visible image of the objective contradictions of man/woman in the bourgeois capitalist world, an image of an alienated condition. The main-taining of the 'good half' involves allowing the 'bad half' to come more and more to the fore, showing that giving is only possible when a profit has been achieved. The 'good half' is affected by this, because the 'bad half' is out to separate her from those she wants to help: the family is given up to the police, the old folk betrayed. Hence the good person is isolated through the acts of the

41

bad one. Shen Te's goodness becomes purely private, as for example her love for her unborn child. The bad Shui Ta becomes more and more public, effacing the good Shen Te.

The isolation of goodness is thus shown to facilitate the rise of the bourgeois: the trader turns capitalist. The commodity man/ woman is worth less than the commodity for which he or she works (cf. *The Measures Taken*). The poor become cheap labour, guaranteeing Shen Te a comfortable life. The answer to the question of the gods, 'what has business to do with a righteous and worthy life?' (*GW* 4, p. 1530), is that such a life in the present world is only available if you have a good business, another dialectical challenge.

The rise of Shen Te is parallel to the rise of Sun, her lover, and to the decline of his love for her. At the beginning of the play Sun is unemployed and belongs to the *Lumpenproletariat*. But as a pilot he can get work which seems satisfying, because flying an aeroplane signifies human aspiration: 'One of us at least shall fly over all this misery, one at least shall rise above us all' (p. 1538). Yet Sun cannot choose the conditions for his flights: he is ordered to fly at night when nothing can be seen. His work turns out to be alienated labour after all; he is employed by a swindler, who hires him out to the highest bidder. Thus Sun's 'private self' is corrupted, like that of Shen Te. He too is caught in a set of contradictions: he can only give himself up to love if he gives up his job (p. 1542). Flying, however, does not only signify a job, it also signifies technical progress, a new future in the twentieth century (cf. Brecht's play *The Flight over the Ocean* (*Der Ozeanflug*, 1928–9), an achievement to be shared by the collective rather than claimed by the individual, one which calls for a new set of social relations. This is far from the case here: Sun works his sordid way up to become a boss and petit-bourgeois aspirer, who disregards human relations. Shen Te is finally saved from a marriage which would have deprived her of both her money and her man. This epitomizes the comic element in bourgeois marriage, in which the individual believes s/he can maintain his or her freedom playing the humanist in private while living in an inhuman society in public. Yet the end of the play is tragic only if the audience forgets about the experiment and gets lost in mimesis, ignoring the fact that Shen Te/Shui Ta is one person (like Anna 1 and Anna 2 in *The Seven Deadly Sins*).

The experimental nature of the play reveals itself in comic replay, repetition and the range of its V-effects, and, in particular, the use of songs and of flashbacks. The songs have a parabolic function; they make use of metaphors which turn out to be literal. The tobacco business is built on smoke, which dissolves into nothing: 'The Song of the Smoke' (p. 1507) is about the family who has sold the business and now has no hope, as well as Shen Te's hopes of love, which also depend on the smoke of the tobacco business. 'The Song of the Water-Seller in the Rain' (pp. 1526 and 1587) likewise follows the economic developments in the play. In Scene 3 Shen Te buys water despite the fact that there is plenty of rain, because she wants to celebrate her love of Sun by a good deed. Scene 9 shows the alienated relationship of Sun and Shen Te (as Shui Ta), and this time Shen Te does not buy any water. This song is an economic parable. For the water-seller, rain is not one of nature's blessings because the exchange value of the commodity he is selling (water) is thereby made valueless. For him there is a crisis of surplus production, solved in the capitalist world by getting rid of the surplus product, in order to make sure of the profit: the consumer pays the higher price. For the small trader, however, this means ruin. Yet this ruin is not something inevitable, since it is the economic laws which determine the value of an object.

This is a play, then, which is riddled with contradictions, encouraging a dialectical approach on the part of the audience. What, then, was its reception?

> Is *The Good Person of Setzuan* a political drama? Do we have to measure it by political criteria, fit it into a political slot? We can and we may, but we don't have to. And that this is so, indicates the highest praise. (*Die Tat*, 1943; in Wyss, 1977, p. 221)

> *The Good Person of Setzuan* happens to be a parable, a *Lehrstück*, that seems once more to owe something to the young Brecht's polemical theory of the 'epic theatre' (today the writer is in the latter half of his forties). It is to be hoped that the shabby outline of this theory, put forward by a youthfully unconcerned anti-Lessingite, is now only intended as a literary reminiscence, printed in the programme notes of the theatre. From this grey, or rather, grisly theory, we prefer to turn to the golden tree of life, Brecht's new piece. (*Neue Züricher Zeitung*, 1943; in Wyss, 1977, p. 223)

The first review goes on to distinguish between political playwrights (*politische Dichter*) and playwriting politicians (*dichtende*

Politiker) (a free translation to make the point). The reviewer
asserts that in the case of the former (which includes Brecht) the
political is transcended, *'aufgehoben'* in Hegel's sense, 'preserved in
its depth, challenged by the process of life and made to play an
essential part in the deepest meaning of the work' (*Die Tat*, Wyss,
1977, p. 221). Whatever else this may mean, it certainly does not
include any concept of class conflict, except perhaps in so far as
it refers to playwriting politicians.

However, the point of Brecht's dialectical theatre is that it cannot
help but enact class conflict in its deliberate rehearsing of social
contradictions. For Brecht human joy or misery is not something
above class conflict but closely bound up with it. The human
emotions he analyses are not resolved in traditional heroic postures
but are subjected to a wit which makes them pleasurable, because
it encourages the spectator to view the contradictions as fruitful in
their very absurdity, as necessary if there is to be any shifting from
the old position to a new one. Pleasure comes in adopting that
critical view which picks up the shifts of meaning, be they comic or
tragic (see Chapter 3 for an elaboration of the comic principle). Only
permanence is frightening. To damn Brecht with faint humanist
praise is surely not an adequate response to his provoking practice.

Brecht wrote a series of fragmentary texts (1927–32), put
together under the title *Jottings on the Dialectical Drama* (*GW* 15, pp.
211–25). The first sketch, 'What might dialectics be?', discusses
the problem of what can in fact be expected of the spectator.
Nowadays, he writes, it seems to be the case that the theatre banks
on the *innocence* of the spectator:

> From the standpoint of the new theatre there would really be
> little against the spectator's adopting a naive attitude, if such an
> attitude were possible. We will here be discussing the fact that
> this is impossible and why it is impossible. Given that it is
> impossible, the spectator must be required to take the (more
> awkward) way of learning something before he turns up at the
> theatre. The spectator should be 'in the picture', prepared,
> 'learned'.[16]

The spectator should be ready to have human material 'thrown at
him' and sort it out for himself. Only those with no scientific
curiosity at all would be unable to see that in the plays the very
lack of clarity itself represents the uncertain and shifting relations
between people: 'the relations of people in our time are unclear'
(*GW* 15, p. 221).

It is the task of the theatre to find a form to present this lack of clarity in as classical a mode as possible, that is, keeping an epic distance. But it requires a particular kind of spectator for the performance to be successful: 'The spectator, drawn into the theatrical event, becomes theatricalized. Hence less goes on *in him* than *with him*' (p. 222). Brecht's refunctioning of the stage thus articulates a praxis grounded in a distinctly modern understanding and designed to open up a new discourse about writer, text, and audience.

Notes

1

> Diese kritische Haltung des Zuschauers (und zwar dem Stoff gegenüber) darf nun nicht etwa als eine rein rationale, rechnerische, neutrale, wissenschaftliche Haltung angesehen werden. Sie muss eine künstlerische, produktive, genussvolle Haltung sein. Sie repräsentiert in der Kunst die praktisch gewordene Kritik der Menschheit an der Natur, auch an der eigenen Natur. . . . Diese neue, neugierige, aktive, erfinderische Haltung ist, wie ich glaube, an Bedeutung, Umfang und Lustgehalt der alten aristotelischen Kartharsis keineswegs unterlegen. (*GW* 15, p. 275)

2 Brecht's use of the term *Umfunktionierung* was enthusiastically taken up by Benjamin (1982) and elaborated by him as 'the transformation of forms and instruments of production by a progressive intelligentsia – an intelligentsia interested in liberating the means of production, and hence active in the class struggle' (1982, p. 93; see also Chapter 4 of this book, p. 79). Brecht uses the term in connection with the cinema, in particular with his own involvement in the filming of *The Threepenny Opera*, a project he conceived as a 'sociological experiment' and over which he went to court, because the film company altered his subversive film script beyond recognition (see *GW* 18, pp. 139–209). For Brecht the film offered a unique chance of transforming the apparatus of production: the film, he argued, was technically in such a primitive state and ideologically so entrapped in mimesis that it afforded an excellent opportunity for intervention. The film director had to be alerted to the fact that it was precisely these shortcomings of his apparatus that could be an advantage because they presuppose a 'refunctioning' (*Umfunktionierung*) of the film: 'the technique of the film is a technique that can make a something out of a nothing' (p. 175).

3

> Das Theater, dass wir in unserer Zeit politisch werden sahen, war vordem nicht unpolitisch gewesen. Es lehrte die Welt so anschauen, wie die herrschenden Klassen sie angeschaut haben wollten . . . die

Welt konnte und musste nunmehr dargestellt werden als eine in Entwicklung begriffene und zu entwickelnde, ohne dass dieser Entwicklung durch irgend eine Klasse Grenzen gesetzt wurden, welche diese in ihrem Interesse für nötig fand. Die passive Haltung des Zuschauers, die der Passivität der überwiegenden Mehrheit des Volkes im Leben überhaupt entsprochen hatte, wich einer aktiven. (*GW* 15, p. 358)

4 'Ein *Gestus* zeichnet die Beziehungen von Menschen zueinander. Eine Arbeitszurichtung zum Beispiel ist kein Gestus, wenn sie nicht eine gesellschaftliche Beziehung enthält wie Ausbeutung oder Kooperation' (*GW* 16, p. 753).

5 In reconstructing the *Fabel* of Brecht's plays I was greatly aided by the accounts given in Knopf's (1980) *Brecht-Handbuch*.

6

Die Welt ist arm, der Mensch ist schlecht.
Wir wären gut, anstatt so roh
Doch die Verhältnisse, sie sind nicht so.
            (*GW* 2, p. 432; *CP* 1, p. 34, adapted)

7

Und der Haifisch, der hat Zähne
Und die trägt er im Gesicht
Und Macheath, der hat ein Messer
Doch das Messer sieht man nicht.
            (*GW* 2, p. 385; *CP* 1, p. 3)

8

Denn wovon lebt der Mensch? Indem er stündlich
Den Menschen peinigt, auszieht, anfällt,
abwürgt und frisst.   (*GW* 2, p. 458; *CP* 1, p. 55)

9

Die Vorführung des Strassendemonstranten hat den Charakter der Wiederholung. Das Ereignis hat stattgefunden, hier findet die Wiederholung statt . . . das Geprobte am Spiel tritt voll in Erscheinung, das auswendig Gelernte am Text, der ganze Apparat und die ganze Vorbereitung. (*GW* 16, p. 548)

10

Für unseren Strassendemonstranten bleibt der *Charakter* des zu Demonstrierenden eine Grösse, die er nicht völlig auszubestimmen hat. Innerhalb gewisser Grenzen kann er so und so sein, das macht nichts aus. Den Demonstranten interessieren seine unfallerzeugenden und unfallverhindernden Eigenschaften. (*GW* 16, p. 551)

11

Es wird jetzt der Versuch gemacht, vom *epischen* Theater zum *dialektischen* Theater zu kommen. Unseres Erachtens und unserer

Ansicht nach waren die Praxis des epischen Theaters und sein ganzer Begriff keineswegs undialektisch, noch wird ein dialektisches Theater ohne das epische Element auskommen. Dennoch denken wir an eine ziemlich grosse Umgestaltung. (*GW* 16, p. 923)

12

Welche Technik es dem Theater gestattet, die Methode der neuen Gesellschaftswissenschaft, die materialistische Dialektik, für seine Abbildungen zu verwerten. Diese Methode behandelt, um auf die Beweglichkeit der Gesellschaft zu kommen, die gesellschaftlichen Zustände als Prozesse und verfolgt diese in ihrer Widersprüchlichkeit. Ihr existiert alles nur, indem es sich wandelt, also in Uneinigkeit mit sich selbst ist. Dies gilt auch für Gefühle, Meinungen und Haltungen der Menschen, in denen die jeweilige Art ihres gesellschaftlichen Zusammenlebens sich ausdrückt. (*GW* 16, p. 682; Willett, 1964, p. 193)

13

Die Darstellungen des bürgerlichen Theaters gehen immer auf die Verschmierung der Widersprüche, auf die Vortäuschung von Harmonie, auf die Idealisierung aus. Die Zustände werden so dargestellt, als könnten sie gar nicht anders sein. . . . Wo es Entwicklung gibt, ist sie nur stetig, niemals sprunghaft, und immer sind es Entwicklungen in einem ganz bestimmten Rahmen, der niemals gesprengt werden kann. (*GW* 16, p. 706; Willett, 1964, p. 277)

14

Mehr oder wenig fertig mit KLEINES ORGANON FÜR DAS THEATER; es ist eine kurze Zusammenfassung des MESSING-KAUFS. Hauptthese: dass ein bestimmtes lernen das wichtigste vergnügen unseres zeitalters ist, so dass es in unserm theater eine grosse stellung einnehmen muss. Auf diese weise konnte ich das theater als ein ästhetisches unternehmen behandeln, was es mir leichter macht, die diversen neuerungen zu beschreiben. Von der kritischen haltung gegenüber der gesellschaftlichen welt ist so der makel des unsinnlichen, negativen, unkünstlerischen genommen, den die herrschende ästhetik ihm aufgedrückt hat. (*AJ*, 18.8.48, p. 518)

15

Ich fühle diese Besonderheit meines Interesses so stark, dass ich mir wie ein Mensch vorkomme, der, sagen wir, als Messinghändler zu einer Musikkapelle kommt und nicht etwa eine Trompete, sondern bloss Messing kaufen möchte. Die Trompete des Trompeters besteht aus Messing, aber er wird sie kaum als Messing verkaufen wollen, nach dem Wert des Messings, als soundso viel Pfund Messing. So aber suche ich hier nach meinen Vorfällen unter Menschen, welche ihr hier irgendwie nachahmt, wenn eure

47

Nachahmungen freilich einen ganz anderen Zweck haben als den, mich zu befriedigen. Klipp und klar: Ich suche ein Mittel, Vorgänge unter Menschen zu bestimmten Zwecken nachgeahmt zu bekommen, höre, ihr verfertigt solche Nachahmungen, und möchte nun feststellen, ob ich diese Art Nachahmungen brauchen kann. (*GW* 16, p. 507; Willett, 1965, pp. 15–16)

16

Nun wäre vom Standpunkt des neuen Theaters aus gegen eine naive Einstellung des Zuschauers wenig zu sagen, wenn eine solche möglich wäre. Es wird davon zu reden sein, dass sie unmöglich ist und warum sie unmöglich ist. Ist sie aber unmöglich, dann muss vom Zuschauer verlangt werden, dass er den (unbequemeren) Weg beschreitet, etwas zu lernen, bevor er im Theater sich einfindet. Dann muss der Zuhörer 'im Bilde', vorbereitet, 'gelehrt' sein. (*GW* 15, p. 211)

3

Theory in praxis: comedy as discourse

Brecht's play *The Exception and the Rule* opens with a prologue, in which the actors appeal to the audience to give their considered attention to the narrative to come:

Examine carefully the behaviour of these people:
Find it surprising though not unusual
Inexplicable though normal
Incomprehensible though it is the rule.
Consider even the most insignificant, seemingly simple
Action with distrust. Ask yourself whether it is necessary
Especially if it is usual.
We ask you expressly to discover
That what happens all the time is not natural.[1]

Has the challenge to the natural anything to do with comedy? Might one derive something from Brecht's dialectical theatre which could contribute to a general theory of the comic, even though he has had little to say directly on the subject?

For Brecht the comic is a historically bound phenomenon, something that can be used for immediate political purposes. His dialectical theatre focuses on what has become comic at a certain moment in history and has now become an anachronism. This is different from the view that regards the comic as an innate quality, with its corollary that there is a genre called comedy. Such a view can only be an idealization of a specific historical situation. The very term 'social comedy', for instance, presupposes that comedy springs from eternal human vanities seen as part and parcel of an immutable human nature. For Brecht, comedy 'quotes' what has never been 'natural'. It is laughter at the 'not natural' which provides the leverage to escape the ideological determinations of

49

society. Brecht finds the source of comedy in the nature of society rather than in the 'nature' of the individual.

Traditional dramatic theory has always tried to keep comedy and tragedy apart: 'All tragedies are finished by death,/All comedies are ended by a marriage' (Byron, *Don Juan*, III, ix). This assumes that death is a given misery and marriage a given happiness, thus creating a discourse which tries to naturalize a particular social order and endow it with the inevitability of a nature assumed to be purposive. This is precisely the view that the Brechtian discourse strives assiduously to undermine. What gives Brecht's theory revolutionary potential is that it is an attack on any reified system, whereas the function of comedy in general has been to maintain the existing established system.

What Brecht calls the 'socially comic', as distinct from the 'eternal comic' (*Theaterarbeit*, 1952, p. 42) is not the same as social comedy, for it is not concerned with criticizing the conventions of a particular age.[2] The intention is not to give vent to laughter as a so-called universal phenomenon, but rather to direct it at the amusement of an audience which is learning to perceive its historical advantage. The target of comedy is the historical irrelevance and inauthentic modes of living of a society stuck with an outworn set of beliefs long after history has moved on. For Brecht the pleasure derived from this undertaking comes from a lively growing consciousness that there is a moment when the dialectic is working in favour of change and transformation, that the comic could thus become an instrument for social change.

The main implication of this principle is that there is no absolute comic or absolute tragic: a failed encounter with history can result in either comedy or tragedy or both. Brecht's plays do not fit traditional notions of two genres called comedy or tragedy, for it is the historical context which determines whether a sequence of events is to be written or read as a comic or tragic narrative. These categories are not to be regarded as mutually exclusive, as essences which can be reconciled, as in tragi-comedy, but as something intertwined in an ambivalent way: the comic combines with the serious when their connection with social and historical realities is revealed. The literary separation of them into two genres is itself an ideological act.

Estrangement and comedy

So how does Brecht go about de-stabilizing the consoling oppositions of our ideological representation of the world? The V-effect,
Brecht's principal instrument for estranging the 'natural', makes
the dialectical nature of the world representable: that is its task.
Brecht's theatre is a practice where the self-reflexivity of the
theatre, its constant disturbance of the spectator's gaze, points to
life as a dialectic, a continual battle of gazes to be fought out
beyond the bounds of the theatre.

What is the relation of estrangement to the comic? They are by
no means one and the same thing, for estrangement can make an
object appear as either tragic or comic, both being contingently
present and by no means exclusive. In a scene in Kurosawa's film
Ran, his version of *King Lear*, the Lord Hidetora is shown running
very fast across a plain with very short jerky running steps, quite
inappropriate for an old man, more reminiscent of a child and
therefore comic, because a child would not have had the motor
capacity to run like that. No one outside a race track would have
run in this way. This displacement of the normal act of running
by a combination of the skill of an athlete with that of an old
man/child running in extreme anguish and terror, from nothing
into nothing, uses a comic effect for a tragic situation, and
moreover exhibits to the spectator's gaze both the already
estranged object Hidetora, with his combination of petulant
childishness and brutal callousness, and a power system, which
although shaky, is by no means such an anachronism in our
present age, and therefore, according to Kurosawa-Brecht, an
invitation to a critical look at prevailing power structures.

Brecht goes beyond past theatrical tradition in which persons
and events were made to look strange, but only in the sense of
being stylized and ritualized, without intervention being invited.
Such stylization is a way of reiterating the myths of a pre-existing
social system, whose objects are safely classified. Brecht points out
the contrary, that the objects in the world are already estranged,
but we do not notice it as long as they serve our immediate
purposes. No object is what language says it is, as Michel Foucault
(1983) makes clear in his discussion of Magritte's picture, *This is
not a Pipe*. The caption reminds you that it is only a representation, and that appearances are fooling you. The comic or tragic
turn of the object is always a latent possibility, made manifest and
palpable to the Brechtian spectator, who is made to observe the

real effects of the objectifications in all their estrangement which produce and control him. Comedy or tragedy are the result of the characters showing this estrangement by means of gestic acting, through which they continue to play the part of split subjects. The Brechtian *gestus* is the calculated pose whereby the actor shows the character's estrangement from the role assigned to him; he does this by producing a set of contradictory attitudes, gestures, and modes of speech which reveal the difference *within* the subject, his being for himself as against his being for others, who confront him similarly divided. For the estrangement is not only of objects but of subjects also; the play of dialectical contradictions in language does not discriminate between the two.

Brecht's utopian wish was to produce an audience who would rejoice at the contradictions of a necessarily estranged world – the uncanniness of a world in flux, the constant shifting of figure and ground in a dialectical movement:

> The theatre of the scientific age is in a position to make dialectics into a source of enjoyment. The unexpectedness of logically progressive or zigzag development, the instability of circumstance, the joke of contradictions and so forth: all these are ways of enjoying the liveliness of men, things and processes, and they heighten both our capacity for life and our pleasure in it.[3]

For Brecht it is scientifically justifiable to analyse intersubjectivity by means of experiments in the theatre, and if it is found that human interaction is essentially ironic in its effects, then comedy and tragedy are contingently present and by no means exclusive. In tragedy the switch of intentions comes too late; in comedy there is time to abandon one set of intentions and accept another. Brecht's conscious endeavour is to encourage the spectator to re-read any tragic happenings enacted on the stage and endow them with the mechanisms of comedy, to see the possibility of the transformation of the one into the other. It is with this purpose that in *The Good Person of Setzuan* he combines the 'good person's' despairing cry, the hasty departure of the gods on a pink cloud, and a brisk address to the audience to think again (*GW* 4, pp. 1606–7).

In Brecht's theatre comedy resides in a constant element of surprise, not only because the unexpected turns up within the expected, but also because the two can exist alongside each other. In *Puntila and his Servant Matti* (*Herr Puntila und sein Knecht Matti*,

1940–8), the wealthy landowner Puntila is unexpectedly genial in
what he takes as his normal state, that of drunkenness, and
expectedly tyrannical in his periodic fits of 'utterly senseless
sobriety' ('totaler sinnloser Nüchternkeit', *GW* 4, p. 1616). He is
not a bad capitalist estranged from his 'natural' goodness: unlike
Shen Te in *The Good Person of Setzuan* he is rich enough to be able
to afford his spasmodic generosity. He makes so much money
when he is sober he can afford to give it away when he is drunk.
But his enlightened chauffeur Matti is more impressed by a proper
work contract than by the whims of his master's 'normal' sentimental state of drunkenness. When Matti is offered Puntila's
daughter Eva in marriage, he conducts a series of tests to see
whether she is suitable to become the wife of a working man. The
estrangement effect resides in the princess having to undergo a
test, instead of, as in 'normal' legend, the prince. Not the prince,
but the princess is found wanting, which goes to show that no
legend is to be taken for granted. Comedy is thus used for an
immediate political purpose, that of disturbing the interpretative
procedures of the characters and through them, the audience. The
landowner's daughter does not share the same sign-system as the
chauffeur: she is indignant, for instance, at his approving pat on
her behind. The chauffeur, on the other hand, is himself bound
by certain class expectations of the function of a spouse.

Brecht asks why a play like *Puntila and his Servant Matti*, about
a feudal conflict between an estate-owner and a worker, still has
relevance: he answers that one can learn, not only from conflict,
but from the history of conflict. Any victory gained will teach
lessons for the future, as long as new systems of oppression go on
replacing the old (*GW* 17, p. 1175). In the Prologue to the play
Puntila is introduced as a 'certain prehistoric animal', a kind of
biological aberration, which is slow to die out. What is comic is
that the species has not yet become extinct. The estrangement
effect is thus no mere device, existing in a vacuum, but is directed
at a specific content, that of oppressor and oppressed. This is
particularly apparent in the scene where the drunken Puntila and
his servant Matti are in the landowner's library and Puntila
instructs Matti to build him a mountain, 'so that I can show you
what a fine country it is you live in . . . shall we climb the Hatel
mountain, Matti . . . we could do it in spirit. We could do it with
the help of a few chairs' (*GW* 4, p. 1704). Matti is encouraged to
demolish valuable furniture to add to the chairs so that the
necessary height is achieved, but is reproached for not having the

right objective: 'you just want to build a mountain that isn't worth
it, one that doesn't offer me a view and doesn't give me any
pleasure, because, see, you're only bent on getting work, I have
to redirect it into useful channels.' The useful channel, ostensibly
showing Matti what a great place Finland is, turns out to be a
celebration of Puntila's property, 'nature' as far as the eye can
see: almost imperceptibly the sky, the clouds drifting in the
Finnish breezes, the wild swans, the fish in the lakes, the cows in
the verdant fields, the mass of birch trees, turn into culture, which
is not lost on Matti who responds thus to the question of whether
he has no love for his fatherland: 'My heart leaps up, when I
behold your forests, Herr Puntila' (p. 1707). Puntila gazes out at
his riches in culture and offers these to Matti as nature. The
concrete sham of the Hatel mountain built up from chairs and
broken bits of furniture provides a new gestalt for that ideological
given we call nature. But Matti is far from trapped in the master's
context: after this scene, the penultimate one in the play, he finally
leaves his employment.

In *The Threepenny Opera* the changing of the context round the
sign is similarly the principal mode of estrangement. The most
successful capitalist is a charity organizer, and his trained group of
tramps and vagabonds join the business in order to milk the very
system that made them what they are, just as is the case with
Mother Courage. The dramatic discourse stages the institutional
conditions and in reproducing them in a variety of contexts reveals
incongruities from a variety of angles. Comedy – and tragedy – are
thus variable outcomes, depending on what myths Brecht chooses
to operate with as part of his game. In *The Threepenny Opera* the royal
messenger as *deus ex machina* completes the mythic presentation of
capitalism in order to estrange the ideology of myths, revealing in
a comic effect the way myths serve to safeguard a society's or
nation's image of itself. In *Mother Courage*, on the other hand,
various mythic virtues, notably that of 'courage', are deconstructed
and shown to contribute to the tragic effects of the play. The V-
effect undermines the inherently comic and interrupts the interpretative procedures by which we single out the comic, preventing
us from laughing with Olympian detachment. Comedy does not
simply come from human vanities or obtuseness, but from ironic
contradictions in the attitudes of people, attitudes which are socially
constructed. The bourgeois can only live within him-/herself as a
split subject, which sometimes produces comic effects (*Man is Man*),
sometimes tragic effects (*Mother Courage*), sometimes both (*The Good*

Person of Setzuan). Brecht's comedy estranges the sign from the thing, or as he would put it, the representation (*die Abbildungen*) from that which is being represented (*das Abgebildete*), that which always eludes representation on account of the 'instability of circumstances':

> The changeability of the world resides in its contradictions. There is something in things, people, circumstances, which simultaneously make them into what they are and what they are not. For they develop, don't stay the same, alter to the point of unrecognizability. And the things, as they happen to be at the moment, contain in themselves, so 'unrecognizably', what is other, earlier, hostile to the present.[4]

The aim of estrangement is to construct an audience which will recognize the dialectical process in all social existence and rise to the challenge of becoming actively and politically engaged. So what is wrong with the usual audience?

Disturbing the gaze

There is a story told by a director of the Berliner Ensemble (Wekwerth, 1980, pp. 114–15). While working with a drama school in Sweden he conducted an experiment, in which he asked the least gifted student to go on to the stage and do nothing either in the way of acting or thinking; the others were asked to guess what it was that their colleague was showing. The curtain was slowly raised and the lights were dimmed. There was a very long silence while the poor fellow just stood there, doing nothing at all. After some five to ten minutes someone began to laugh and the laughter carried on for five minutes, followed by a period of deep gloom. Eventually the curtain came down and the audience was asked to comment on what it had seen. They said they had experienced the tragedy of man in the age of technology, his loneliness and alienation. They had admired the courage of his resistance, his refusal to compromise, his total command of the situation, all splendidly acted. But then they had laughed when it became obvious that this completely inflexible man, while quite unaware of what was going on around him in the city, was making a great show of refusal, superbly acted. Finally they had felt great sadness on account of the plight of the individual in Sweden. Whereupon the director told them that nothing at all had been performed.

This story demonstrates the tendency of any audience to impose their gaze on the stage happenings. The blank gaze of the other served as an invitation to empathize and to transfer to the figure on the stage whatever fantasies collectively moved them. The gaze has the power to rouse unconscious motivation and intention. To feel a gaze is to make oneself an object of that gaze, precisely what Brecht wants to stop. According to Lacan (1977a) the lure of the gaze is first discovered in the mirror-stage of early life, before there is a symbolic eye to represent the subject. At that time the subject deludes itself that it exists in an unbroken unity with its mirror-image, and its relation to other objects in the world will be determined by that first narcissistic and imaginary relation with this apparently unified image. From then on seeing and idealizing will be functions tied to the power of the gaze, denying all separation and difference. The narcissistic subject will tirelessly continue to search for itself in the other, but the other will surprise it by having a desire of his or her own. Thus continuous perception is disorganized by another's gaze, a kind of built-in estrangement effect, which constitutes a 'dialectic of the eye and the gaze' (Lacan, 1977b, p. 102) – 'the eye' as caught up in the Symbolic Order of language and 'the gaze' as lingering in the Imaginary realm of the mirror-stage, pursuing a narcissistic fantasy. Lacan sees this as a universal black comedy, where lack paves the way to desire – the other has not got what I want so I must look beyond to the Symbolic Order and a provisional name and role – and lack is simultaneously a threat to narcissism and the desire for a safe identity. Hence the continuing search for a reinforcing mirror-image.

Where the realist theatre relying on illusion actually invites the spectator's gaze and encourages him to read the proffered text naively, as a mirror-image of a pre-existing world, the self-referential theatricality of Brecht's theatre, with its constant reminders of the illusory and hence changeable nature of the world, produces an engagement with the theatrical in life. The spectator-subject is also being theatricalized, for he is made to play a role, that of being seen seeing. The luridly illuminated paper moon, appearing with the caption 'Don't be such a romantic gawper!' ('Glotzt nicht so romantisch', *GW* 1, p. 70) in a play which deconstructs romantic love, reminds the onlooker that he is being observed and cannot simply impose a master-gaze. His gaze is an object of seeing, at the same time as it is engaged in seeing:[5]

We must always remember that the originality of the Brechtian sign is that it is *to be read twice over*: what Brecht gives us to read is, by a kind of disengagement, the reader's gaze, not directly the object of his reading; for this object reaches us only by the act of intellection (an alienated act) of a first reader who is already on the stage. (Barthes, 1986, p. 219)

The voyeuristic gaze of the spectator is thereby turned into a symbolic eye: he is forced to acknowledge his split subject-hood and shown that he too is part-object, part-subject.

Brecht uses comic effects to disrupt the gaze and open the symbolic eye of the spectator. He does this both on the stage, where anything, animate or inanimate, can become a gaze, disrupting the equanimity, first, of the characters on the stage, and, second, of the spectator. The stage solicits the gaze of the spectator by entrapping his gaze in the gazes of those on the stage and then breaking the mirror of identification. Suddenly the text reads her, him, or you. Both characters and audience are constantly given visual and verbal shocks of surprise, and hence Barthes writes 'Better than a semiology, what Brecht leaves us with is a seismology' (Barthes, 1986, p. 214). The character of Puntila, for instance, is a veritable trap for the gaze on account of his jolly drunkenness, not only for the spectator but also for actor and author:

The main problem of the actor playing the role of Puntila is in the presentation of the drunkenness, which makes up nine-tenths of his part. He should achieve the effect of being repulsive and unpleasant when he goes in for the expected reelings about of the drunkard on the stage, thus revealing the drugged condition which blurs and devalues all physical and spiritual states.[6]

Stekel [the actor] acted Puntila in Zürich before he appeared in Berlin. In Zürich he played him as though without a mask, and most of the spectators gathered the impression that he was a genial human being with a few unpleasant waverings in his state of sobriety, which took on the character of a hangover, so much so that these waverings seemed forgivable. In Berlin, having learned from this effect, he chose a repulsive-looking bald head and made himself up with jaded and dissolute features. Only now did his charm when he was drunk have a dangerous effect, his way of accosting people socially became that of a crocodile.[7]

The apparently proffered identification, the human-all-too-human countenance, needs to be brutally disturbed. An excellent essay on the play (Hermand, 1977) shows the temptation offered to the spectator to lose himself in the richness of mythical elements – rich estate-owner, beautiful daughter, faithful servant – and to take the Puntila/Matti relation as a feat of sheer invention, as a triumph of the comic over the political. This is the option that the reader cannot take: Puntila, far from being split into a 'bad' sober half and a 'good' drunken half, as he likes to project himself, is a persona produced by the socio-economic world, in which his drunken self produces sentimental effects and his sober self produces brutal effects, each half estranging the other. Puntila is as much, if not more, of a threat when he is drunk, for his common touch enables him to manipulate all the better. Neither drunk nor sober self will serve as a model, since drunkenness will not change the world, and the world as it is seems incapable of producing an acceptable sober self.

Brecht countermands the identification of the spectator with a 'good' and 'bad' Puntila by the way he organizes stage gazes and objects in order to entrap the audience's gaze. 'The theatrical is structured by the gaze of the other' (McLeod, 1980, p. 19). Brecht's stage effects are designed to involve the spectator's gaze with those of certain actors or sets of actors, thus referring the spectator back to the theatrical production. The 'chauffeur' Matti (the one who steers) is the one who ends up staging a considerable variety of scenes which bring to light the class conflict governing the play. Prior to the scene where Matti puts Eva on trial as a prospective wife she endeavours to lure him into a flirtation. For a moment Matti's seductive gaze is on Eva, until he sees (with his symbolic eye) her calculating one. The audience sees Eva's attempts to engage Matti's sexual interest, as written in the stage directions: 'Enter Eva, holding a cigarette tip yards long, copying a seductive gait she has seen in the cinema' (*GW* 4, p. 1658), and observes Matti's dawning perception of the way in which she wishes to produce the scene. He loses interest in her proposal of a nocturnal expedition to catch lobsters when he understands that this particular lobster does not intend to be caught in this way. His symbolic eye records the class-consciousness which curtails her tentative seductive offer. He recognizes himself as a production of her desire (to catch real lobsters, with the proper tools, while conducting an imaginary flirtation in which he catches nothing) and he declines the offer. The audience's gaze is on both of them, learning by means of such internal structures of seeing, rather than through the consciousness of a single character.

Matti is an adept in soliciting the gaze of the spectator by the games he plays, showing that the slave can play, whereas the master cannot. He is master in the game, who is finally not trapped in the master's gaze (he gives in his notice), but develops a symbolic eye for the missing third term, the economic and political conditions which determine the system in which Puntila can only play 'drunk' and 'sober'. The spectator sees all that Matti sees and more: he comes to recognize himself as a production and to see the part that representation plays in the fictive formation of the self. His passive consuming gaze is turned into an active critical eye. The theatrical can thus produce a disturbance within the political consciousness of the spectator. This disturbance is not merely a correction of error, replacing a false view with a true one, but a realization that ideology avails itself of an essentially dramatic form (as when the subject confronts itself in Lacan's mirror phase). What implications might this have for a new theory of comedy?

The comic return of the repressed

The socially-comic

For plays like 'Puntila' one is not likely to find all that much in the lumber room of the 'Eternal Comic'. Although the 'Eternal Comic' – the clown who marches out of the room with great aplomb and falls on his nose – also has a social aspect, yet this has got lost, so that the clown's fall appears as something biological, something that is comic in all persons and all circumstances. The actors who perform 'Puntila and his Servant Matti' must derive the comical from the present-day class situation, even when the members of this class or that do not laugh.[8]

The appeal of the clown is in his forever earnestly striving and forever unexpectedly failing to fulfil the role society has imposed on him; his conscientious desire to play the social role comes inevitably to grief, and therein lies his general 'biological' appeal, namely that the mind's plans can never anticipate all the body's needs. In *The Baden Learning-Play on Consent* (*Das Badener Lehrstück vom Einverständnis*, 1929) there is a clown scene in which three

59

clowns perform: two small ones 'help' a giant one (with the
ordinary name of Herr Schmidt) by systematically sawing him
apart, limb by limb, to get rid of his aches and pains, until finally
only his torso is left. He unquestioningly accepts his own defeat,
trusting in others' help. This is a different category of clowning
from that of Charlie Chaplin, for the latter, in spite of his sufferings under vested authorities, always outdoes them: the
ambiguities and paradoxes turn out to his advantage, sometimes
accidentally, sometimes as a result of his heroic presence-of-mind.
Tati's M. Hulot, too, is something of an innocent, as someone
whose deference to rank includes a belief in a greater social
harmony than exists in fact, which he, as a lowly functionary, is
trying to uphold and failing signally, while all the while maintaining his serenity. Herr Schmidt, on the other hand, is ideologically
trapped: the ambiguities are working against him and he does not
perceive it. The 'learning-play' supplies the appropriate political
context in the scene that follows, entitled 'The Refusal of Help':

When violence rules no longer, help will no longer be needed.
Thus you ought not to demand help, but abolish violence
instead.
Help and violence make up a whole
And the whole must be transformed.[9]

The example from *The Baden Learning-Play* brings home the
futility of expecting help within a system which is violent and
repressive in its power structure. The scene throws up the question
which makes comedy into a discourse instead of an absolute: who
laughs, from what place, about what, and at whom? For Brecht
society's and history's rigidities are not absolute: his comic praxis
implies an attack on all theories of comedy which assume that
individual and society are opposed givens. Brecht's theatre centres
on the changing of contexts: who has the power to change the
context round the sign? As in Freud's theory of the tendentious
joke (Freud, 1953, VIII, pp. 97–102), the teller of the joke (Brecht)
requires a listener as ally and a third person as object or butt. In
the clown scene of *The Baden Learning-Play* the listener-audience
would be tempted to align himself with the clowns as the author's
satirical weapons, but this option does not last. The audience is
caught out when it becomes increasingly clear that the dismember-
ment of Herr Schmidt is an attack on its own cherished hopes and
beliefs in a system which is supposed to provide relief from suffer-
ing. Brecht, as in Freud's joke theory, is an unscrupulous teller

who has caught the audience out in a complicitous laugh at Herr Schmidt. But whereas Freud only saw the laugh as a temporary lifting of the law's repression and a momentary saving of psychic energy, Brecht wants to channel this energy into changing a law which has produced such a paradoxical bond between help and violence. Something is artificially kept alive to maintain the prevailing order: what is comical is the return of that which no longer serves desire.

Marcuse (1955, p. 44) gave the term 'surplus repression' to those restrictions which are imposed to maintain, not a social system in its corporate struggle with natural scarcity, but a particular hierarchical form of domination concerned to preserve its privileged structure. Even where natural scarcity is overcome with the help of technology, this excess of repression continues to be operative. The *gestus* of Brecht's actors repeats their capture in an anachronistic system which frustrates all communal aspiration, where the subject connives, or is made to connive, at his own castration (see the castration scenes in Brecht's *Man is Man* (*GW* 1, p. 369) and in his re-politicized version of Jakob Lenz's play *The Private Tutor* (*GW* 6, p. 2381). The *gestus* reveals the political repressed as the drive restricted by social class, not as what the bourgeois regards as the sublimation of the drive, or 'self-discipline'. The *gestus* is the desire of the dominant Other in us, which Brecht's theatre strives to deconstruct.

Brecht wishes to make palpable a system of social relations which defeats all creative self–other relationships, a defeat the system itself conceals by its stimulation of wants. In his brief song-ballet *The Seven Deadly Sins of the Petit-Bourgeois*, the seven traditional vices are virtues when viewed from an anti-capitalist standpoint. To demonstrate this, Brecht works with a split subject, the singing Anna I as business manager of the dancing Anna II, the goods being sold. The two are on a tour to raise money for a home for themselves and their family. Anna II begins each scene by refusing to submit to the market economy and this results in a transvaluation of values: she shows laziness in promoting injustice, pride in refusing to make her art saleable, gluttony in the assertion of her natural appetite, lust in the refusal to be calculating about the other, and so on. Where Anna II reveals her subjectivity in dance, Anna I criticizes in song her 'sister's' failure to meet the desire of the capitalist Other. A split is thus enacted and transmitted to the audience. It is a parable of the divide that appears between those who toil to produce the goods and those who consume them. The audience is invited to acknowledge this split.

Brecht's dramaturgy sets out to deconstruct any surplus repression, and to show it up as outdated and comically irrelevant to the social good, thus leaving the reader/audience with contradictions and the task of the resolution of them in life's praxis. The reader/audience is to participate in the fun of making new meaning, participating in the process of 'interventionist thinking'. His was a vast and ambitious undertaking, directed at making available 'the pleasure of the text' not only to the single subject but to the class that was being oppressed. This is not merely a case of changing the political content of art, but of changing the relations between producer and consumer. The spectator's own subjectivity is brought into question along with the representations on the stage; the desires of the body are to be reached so that it awakens to an understanding of its own socialization and the discovery of its political repression.

Towards a Marxist theory of comedy

The function of the comic in Brecht's theatre is thus radically different from the function of the comic in any theatre before Brecht. Although the repetition of self-defeating contradictions has always been a source of comedy, in the past the comic effects thereby produced were interpreted quite differently. Bergson, for instance, assumes a harmonious position, a perfect objectification from which to judge the self-defeat of the other: the living trapped in the mechanical, a combination which amuses him so much, is blamed on the character and has little to do with the fixity of the social order. For Hegel, on the other hand, contrary to Brecht, 'there is nothing comical abut the vices of mankind' (Hegel, tr. T.M. Knox, 1975, 2 vols, II, p. 1200); true comedy occurs when a character perceives the clash and contradiction in his life and proves himself immune to it:

What is comical[10] . . . is a personality or subject who makes his own actions contradictory and so brings them to nothing, while remaining tranquil and self-assured in the process. Therefore comedy has for its basis and starting point what tragedy may end with, namely an absolutely reconciled and cheerful heart. Even if its possessor destroys by the means he uses whatever he wills and so comes to grief in himself because by his own efforts he has accomplished the very opposite of what he aimed at, he still has not lost his peace of mind on that account. (Hegel, 1975, p. 1220)

For Hegel it is comic that the subject is so serenely sure of himself despite the fact that his aims 'have no real substance'. It is precisely the mismatch between the character's aspirations and his own enlightened perception of his lowly place in the world which is for Hegel the essence of the comic. His failure is so endearing because he carries on blithely regardless of his complete and utter irrelevance in the order of things:

> The comical therefore plays its part more often in people with lower views, tied to the real world and the present, i.e. among men who are what they are once and for all, who cannot be or will anything different, and, though incapable of any genuine 'pathos', have not the least doubt about what they are and what they are doing. But at the same time they reveal themselves as having something higher in them because they are not seriously tied to the finite world with which they are engaged but are raised above it and remain firm in themselves and secure in face of failure and loss. (Hegel, 1975, pp. 1220–1)

This hardly amounts to a revolutionary programme. The comic is tied to the lower orders: the underling in comedy has aims above his station and then has to laugh when they come to nought, and we with him, because he has such a firm hold upon his blithe and cheerful universe that he does not care when his cherished misguided aims come to nothing. Hegel misses the dynamic function of the comic as a movement of social antagonisms. He assumes the identity of subject and object, the character's identification with the object that defeats him. Seen from a Brechtian perspective this is tantamount to making the subject collude in his own repression.

In an article on Hegel and the comic, Wolfgang Heise (1964) argues that Hegel, in spite of himself, has seen that the greatness of the comic is rooted in the changes of epochs and social formations. Hegel was the first to bring out the relation of the comic to the age in which it appears. Although he did not see the relation of comedy to class conflict, he understood human activity as proceeding dialectically, through the interplay of labour and necessity. In this he recognized the place of conflict but not its true motivation. He could not ignore this conflict of new and old, acknowledging that the comic hero, even if misdirected, was trying

63

to achieve power, though that power was perhaps not worth having in its existent form.

Hegel sees the dialectical principle in both comedy and tragedy: the tragic hero, trapped by his 'pathos' (those committed desires characterizing his selfhood), the resolution only achieved by eternal justice; the comic hero, blessedly free from this compulsion, rising above defeat serene and self-assured. But whereas for Hegel comedy resides in a person being immune to the contradictions in his life, for Brecht this proves the impossibility of separating comedy from tragedy. What is comic and tragic together is man's repeated attempts to appropriate the very reality which has made him an alienated being.

For Brecht the lower-class characters, even when they are aware of the contradictions, are still caught by them. In *The Exception and the Rule*, one of Brecht's *Lehrstücke*, the Coolie is defeated – to the point of death. The 'rule' is revealed as thoroughly class-determined. The Coolie is in a no-win situation when he offers his last drop of water to his master the Merchant, not as a gesture of benevolence, but with a better understanding of the alienated conditions under which he is working than the master, for he foresees what will happen if he is found alive and his master dead. The Merchant, however, can only see the Coolie as driven by resentment after the ill-treatment he has meted out to him on their joint journey: hence he misinterprets the outstretched hand, first as a gesture of aggression, and second – after the event – as a totally irrational act of kindness, given his treatment of the Coolie. At any rate he shoots the Coolie down in 'self-defence' because, given the circumstances, he had no reason to suppose that the Coolie's action would constitute an exception to the rule, and the Judge subsequently endorses this view. Theoretically speaking, the audience laughs at the Merchant and the Judge for their limited understanding, but practically speaking, the Merchant has won, for he has survived and does not even have to pay damages to the widow of the Coolie. For the Coolie and his widow it is therefore no laughing matter. There is someone to laugh at but no one to laugh with. The situation is undecidably comic and tragic. The question of who laughs, from what place, about what, and at whom cannot thus be decided ontologically. There is no comic essence, only a discourse of power, in which it is up to the public to make sure that in the future it will not be the law which laughs last and longest.

The Exception and the Rule is perhaps the nearest one can get towards an idea for a Marxist theory of comedy. It is a comedy of reification, of subjects caught up in a set of social antagonisms demonstrated with all its tragic implications. Where Hegel believes that the living creativity of Spirit, the Ideal Being of the universe, abandons objective forms when they cease to work towards its own self-realization, Marx sees the dialectical process as a material one and discerns the comic and the supersession of the old objectifications, where this has not yet been noticed. Comedy, according to Marx, is to help people to part 'happily' (*heiter*) from their past (Marx, 1975 edn, p. 248). This is now itself an anachronistic view. Tragedy must be added as a possible alternative: comedy and/or tragedy result when the dialectical contradiction leads to various kinds of self-defeat for the individual and the collective. For Brecht comedy has the function of showing that the future depends on being able to finish with the past, on getting rid of its encrustations and fixities. Self-defeat occurs where characters struggle to appropriate the very reality of their oppressors which has produced them as alienated beings in the first place. This goes for the many split characters so far discussed: Shen Te/Shui Ta, Anna 1 and 2, the Coolie who has internalized the repressive law, Macheath as bourgeois/gangster, Puntila as humanist/tyrant, Courage as mother/merchant. Both comedy and tragedy are selectively constituted by a set of ideological assumptions held at a particular moment in history: something is unwittingly kept alive to maintain the prevailing order. Marx and Brecht, if thus revised, not only relate comedy to history but show that it is the incessant *clash* of objectifications which produce both comedy and tragedy, thus underlining the need for an aesthetic of contradictions rather than one of mimesis. For Brecht and his contemporaries the nature of this aesthetic became a controversial issue which inaugurated a whole series of debates.

Notes

1

> Betrachtet genau das Verhalten dieser Leute:
> Findet es befremdend, wenn auch nicht fremd
> Unerklärlich, wenn auch gewöhnlich
> Unverständlich, wenn auch die Regel.
> Selbst die kleinste Handlung, scheinbar einfach
> Betrachtet mit Misstrauen! Untersucht, ob es nötig ist
> Besonders das Übliche!
> Wir bitten euch ausdrücklich, findet

Das immerfort Vorkommende nicht natürlich!
(*GW* 2, p. 793: *CP* 4i, p. 37)

2 See Giese (1974) whose valuable work first drew my attention to Brecht's coining of this term and led to the insights for its elaboration.

3

Das Theater des wissentschaftlichen Zeitalters vermag die Dialektik zum Genuss zu machen. Die Überraschung der logisch fortschreitenden oder springenden Entwicklung, der Unstabilität aller Zustände, der Witz der Widersprüchlichkeiten und so weiter, das sind Vergnügungen an der Lebendigkeit der Menschen, Dinge und Prozesse, und sie steigern die Lebenskunst sowie die Lebensfreudigkeit. (*GW* 16, p. 702; Willett, 1964, p. 277)

4

Die Veränderbarkeit der Welt besteht auf ihrer Widersprüchlichkeit. In den Dingen, Menschen, Vorgängen steckt etwas, was sie macht, wie sie sind, und zugleich etwas, was sie anders macht. Denn sie entwickeln sich, bleiben nicht, verändern sich bis zur Unkenntlichkeit. Und die Dinge, wie sie eben jetzt sind, enthalten in sich, so 'unkenntlich', anderes Früheres, dem jetzigen Feindliches. (*GW* 16, pp. 925–6)

5 The deployment of stage-gazes in relation to the gaze of the spectator as a theoretical device of the committed playwright, namely Sartre and Brecht, is powerfully argued by McLeod, 1980, to whose insights this chapter is indebted.

6

Der Darsteller des Puntila findet sein Hauptproblem in der Darstellung der Trunkenheit, welche neun Zehntel der Rolle ausmacht. Es müsste abstossend und widerwärtig wirken, wenn er die konventionelle Trunkenheitswalze der Bühne einlegte, das heisst einen Zustand der Vergiftung zeigte, der alle seelischen und körperlichen Vorgänge verwischte und entwertete. (*Theaterarbeit*, 1952, p. 19)

7

Stekel spielte den Puntila in Zürich, bevor er ihn in Berlin spielte. In Zürich spielte er ihn fast ohne Maske, und es entstand bei den meisten Zuschauern der Eindruck eines sympathetischen Menschen mit einigen üblen Anwandlungen im Zustand der Nüchterheit, welche den Charakter des Katzenjammers annahm, so dass auch diese Anwandlungen entschuldigt schienen. In Berlin, belehrt durch diese Wirkung, wählte er einen ekelhaft geformten Kahlkopf und schminkte sich verlebte und niedrig aussehende Züge. Erst jetzt wirkte sein Charm in der Trunkenheit gefährlich, wurden seine Annäherungen zu denen eines Krokodils. (*Theaterarbeit*, 1952, p. 22)

8

Für Stücke wie den 'Puntila' wird man nicht allzuviel in der Rumpelkammer des 'Ewig Komischen' finden. Zwar hat auch das 'Ewig Komische' – der mit grossem Aplomb ausmaschierende Clown fällt auf die Nase – ein gesellschaftliches Element, jedoch ist dieses verlorengegangen, so dass der Clownsturz als etwas schlechthin Biologisches, als bei allen Menschen in allen Situationen Komisches erscheint. Die Schauspieler, die 'Herr Puntila und sein Knecht Matti' spielen, müssen die Komik aus der heutigen Klassensituation ziehen, selbst wenn dann die Mitglieder der oder jener Klasse nicht lachen. (*Theaterarbeit*, 1952, p. 42)

9

Wenn keine Gewalt mehr herrscht, kann Hilfe
verweigert werden
Also sollt ihr nicht Hilfe verlangen, sondern
die Gewalt abschaffen.
Hilfe und Gewalt geben ein Ganzes
Und das Ganze muss verändert werden.
(*GW* 2, p. 599)

10 Knox's translation of the German terms 'komisch' and 'das Komische' as 'comical' presents difficulties in the context of my discussion. In English the word 'comical' is more often used of actual ludicrous situations; according to the Oxford English Dictionary, it means 'mirth-provoking'. The 'comic', on the other hand, is more often used as the general English term for the genre, and it is in this sense that I take Hegel's definition.

4

Placing the theory:
Brecht and modernity

Modernity is the definition, controversially open, of what is to
constitute the character of a present age, in particular its best
perspective upon its future. Modernity refers for us to the period
from about 1880 onwards which ushered in a rebellion against
traditional forms and the beliefs held about them. It may therefore
be taken with regard to the art to include the twin terms of
'modernism' and 'avant-garde'. Since the four theorists under
discussion, Lukács, Brecht, Benjamin, and Adorno, hold different
positions in that rebellion, the distinction is not irrelevant for the
purposes of this analysis. Peter Bürger (1984), in response to
Renato Poggioli (1968), who lumped all the modernists together
under the term 'avant-garde', has argued persuasively that the
move away from the autonomy of art at a time when writers and
artists were being exposed to the effects of a mass-economy started
off regressively as a flight into what became known as Aestheticism, artistic innovation for its own sake, which included an
emphasis on the shock value of art via new forms and devices.
Bürger therefore wants to distinguish between two different
theoretical impulses, two different strategies of negation that
modernism is heir to: modernism as a many-sided attack on traditional artistic procedures (with the Russian Formalist concept of
'defamiliarization' as paradigmatic for the new function of art);
avant-garde as a concerted attack on the institutionalized production and reception of art (Bürger, 1984, pp. 15–27). (The Brechtian concept of *Verfremdung* might here be cited as the key
ideological device.) These differences can be elided only if the
common ground is taken to be the very general one of the
challenge levelled at conventional forms of language. It leaves out
of account the essential point that Aestheticism intensified the

separation of art from bourgeois society and thereby increased its autonomy, whereas avant-gardism tried to return art to a form of social praxis.[1] The confrontation between the four Marxist theorists, Lukács, Brecht, Benjamin, and Adorno, centres on the problem facing the politically committed artist at a time when technological progress was bringing about a radical change in the production and reception of art.

The four protagonists in the ongoing theoretical confrontation about the relation between aesthetics and politics all shaped the future course of what is now known as ideological criticism, that is, the attempt to demystify the notion of art as an autonomous practice, unchanged by the history of its production and reception. It was Brecht who took the offensive in producing and promoting an aesthetic of contradiction which went counter to the more conservative and preservative theories of Lukács and Adorno, whose views on the most appropriate mode of representation for the so-called progressive writer differed sharply from Brecht's. Only Brecht and Benjamin were in agreement with regard to the positive political and ideological function of avant-garde techniques: Lukács and Adorno remained committed, albeit in very different ways, to an art which contained its contradictions within itself, and thereby, in their view, resisted the twin dangers of reification and commodification to which the new techniques seemed to lend themselves.

The Brecht/Lukács dispute

The dispute between Lukács and Brecht centres around their opposed conception of what constitutes a work of realism within a context of declared political struggle, in this case that of Marxism. How might literature and the arts best be enlisted to support such an enterprise, both as regards a productive criticism of past works of realism and as a programme of work for present and future?

For Marxism art has a special task, namely the humanizing of what has become reified. It was Lukács who elaborated the concept of reification, taken from Marx, referring to it as 'the central structural problem of capitalist society' (Lukács, 1971, p. 83). Marx was the first to claim that both the objective world of the product and the institutional relations that the market inevitably induced took on a given rigidified form which seemed real in its own right and beyond the control and criticism of men. The reification of the product as an independent object he named 'commodity fetishism', because he regarded this aspect of reification as a delusion in which imaginary characteristics were being given a thing-like status. Human beings also became fixed in thing-like relations, governing all their social interactions. It was this latter aspect of Marx's theory which Lukács brought into prominence, pointing out that this false objectification worked down into the activity of individuals such that the delusion led to an estrangement from their real potential.

Both Brecht and Lukács wanted to undo the effects of reification under capitalism. For Lukács this was to be done via an art which proclaimed 'totality', a visionary de-reification, a linking of 'concrete' experience with 'abstract' understanding of how this experience could realize itself under present conditions. Lukács builds through Marx on Hegel: the abstract superstructure of thought and culture is in continuing interaction with the concrete world, progressing via the overcoming of contradictions. The evolution is that of material human being; the dialectic arises from concrete experience. For Hegel the concrete world shaped itself according to an evolving abstract idea; for Marx real human beings were able to effect a dialectical advance towards the overthrow of capitalism. The writer's task was to make visible these contradictions between concrete and abstract by a particular mode of representation which for Lukács spelled realism – a kind of mimesis-plus, which 'reflected' an 'objective reality', yet at the same time revealed the causes of its shortcomings.

For Brecht the task of the artist was to de-naturalize the rigidified world by means of a whole new range of formal devices which would draw the spectator's attention to the content of the contradictions under which he/she lived. Lukács, on the other hand, feared that the fragmentation and artificiality of modernist techniques would harden the reader's response to the world and de-sensitize her/him as regards any possibility of achieving a wholesome existence. For him stylization spelt no more than novelty and empty technique. He was quite unable to see how form could point towards a specific content, namely how it could reveal to the spectator that he himself was involved in the production process. In *The Meaning of Contemporary Realism* he condemns the 'oversimplified schema' of Brecht's *The Measures Taken* and subscribes to the humanist view of Brecht as outlined in Chapter 1, maintaining that 'the mature Brecht, by overcoming his earlier, one-sided theories, had evolved into the greatest realistic playwright of his age' (Lukács, 1963, pp. 88 and 89). For Lukács the late Brecht has returned to the classic realist fold and all is forgiven:

> Where Brecht's characters had once been spokesmen for political points of view, they are now multi-dimensional. They are living human beings, wrestling with conscience and the world around them. Allegory has acquired flesh and blood; it has been transformed into a true dramatic typology. Alienation-effect ceases to be the instrument of an artificial, abstract didacticism; it makes possible literary achievement of the highest order. All great drama, after all, must find means to transcend the limited awareness of the characters presented on the stage. (Lukács, 1963, p. 88)

With friends like that, who needs enemies? It did not occur to Lukács that in Brecht's *Lehrstücke* the actors/protagonists themselves work out the dialectic – it does not happen above and beyond them. They step out of a chorus which includes them and rehearse the different roles the drama demands of them in order to test out if 'the text' might be changed (see p. 15 of this book).

Lukács believes that in a work of classic realism the alienation of the individual is transcended by the showing through of the social totality that would break up the existing reification. 'Realistic experience' is false consciousness: what is required is a realism which allows you to see the underlying abstract connections. On the one hand, there is the reified world of lived experience, on the other hand, the totality, the perspective of what it all fits into, allowing you to see the ideological forces which produced the reifications and to transform the reified by seeing its relation to the whole. Lukács is interested in the dialectical character of objective reality. We can only grasp the concrete and accidental parts of reality, those that have become reified in the historical world of capitalism. But these appearances only make up one side of reality: the other side is determined by the dynamic of the world-historical interests of the proletariat. History has produced a distortion in that the alienated subject is made remote from the concrete and can only perceive the world in a rigid and abstract way: only when the concrete phenomena are perceived in the context of the totality – the historical, socio-economic, and material existence – can the subject perceive reality for what it is.

For Lukács, realist writers, such as Balzac or Tolstoy, were historically involved with the bourgeoisie in its emancipatory moments and were thus able to give the reader access to the conflictual currents of history. Fredric Jameson (1974, pp. 160–205), in putting the case for Lukács, comments on some of the historical circumstances which led to Lukács's judgement about which writers qualified for his approval. Whereas Lukács applauds Balzac he disapproves of Zola and Joyce, for, far from having penetrated to the ideological sources of their world, they have been overcome by reification and are giving up by yielding to a fragmentary stream of experience, without including the causes of that fragmentation and thereby showing the possibility of overcoming it. Balzac, as Jameson observes, was more lucky in his historical period (1974, pp. 195 and 203) because he was in at the beginning of capitalism and was able to see everything become reified. Thus he was able to load incident with social meaning, providing narrative within a context of totality. It is the epic style of writing which Lukács fiercely defends and distinguishes from what he considers to be mere factual description (Lukács, 1970, pp. 110–48);

> The inner poetry of life is the poetry of men in struggle, the poetry of the turbulent, active interaction of men. Without this inner poetry to intensify and maintain its vitality, no real epic is possible and no epic composition can be elaborated that will rouse and hold people's interest. (p. 126)

> The decisive ideological weakness of the writers of the descriptive method is in their passive capitulation to these consequences, to these phenomena of fully-fledged capitalism, and in seeing the result but not the struggle of opposing forces. (p. 146)

> Description is the writer's substitute for epic significance which has been lost. (p. 130)

In another essay (Lukács, 1969, pp. 150–8) Lukács criticizes a new novel by Ernst Ottwalt, launching a full-scale attack on the documentary style of narrative employed by the proletarian writer as against the image-making (*Gestaltung*) of the classical realist writer. His declared aim is to put proletarian-revolutionary literature on the right path as regards theory and methodology.[2] Lukács's essay purports to demonstrate the damaging effects of leftist attitudes, which went counter to the official policy of the German Communist Party.[3] Ottwalt, a colleague of Brecht's, is attacked for his documentary style of writing, which fetishizes facts in its combination of documentation with political commentary

(1969, p. 153). Lukács maintains that Ottwalt, far from exposing injustice as he intends, does no more than bleakly reinforce the power of the ideological state apparatus in retailing the facts of the case, for these only represent the empirical surface of things. Though it may not be bad in itself, it is not suitable as a literary method, because it takes a particular instance as an example of a 'fully sensuously re-lived experience, concrete and individual' (1969, p. 154), which then has to be explained in an abstract and didactic manner in order to make it generally applicable. Lukács argues that this is using the methods of science where they are out of place:

> The methods of representation used by science and art differ fundamentally and mutually exclude each other, even though the basic ground for research is the same . . . an 'artistic' representation which has scientific aims will always be a pseudo-science, as well as a pseudo-art. (1969, p. 156)[4]

What kind of theory of representation is it which insists on the classical view that the artist 'portrays' a pre-existent world, selecting from a store of images which are bound to reflect the objective structure of reality, yet seems to want neither 'idealist subjectivism', nor 'photographic naturalism', nor 'idealist objectivism' (Lichtheim, 1970, pp. 124–9)? For Eagleton, Lukács begs the question of the very nature of cognition. He seems to presuppose that the nearer the artist gets to an understanding of the totality as some kind of grand context of relevance, not only will his judgement be nearer the truth but also the more valuable will be the work of art he produces: 'It just is the case that art which gives us the "real" is superior art' (Eagleton, 1981, p. 85).

Brecht, however, uses demystification, not to get at the real, but to get a proper relation to reality, for it is in that relation that human values take their shape. Demystification demonstrates the dialectic in use, forcing the audience to make dialectical moves themselves, and is therefore valuable in itself. By doubting all codes and representations, Brecht reveals the contradictions of history, and this entails playing with the form, disrupting, freezing, and spacing the action, so as to show up the conflictual forces at various levels of the social order. In the elephant-sale episode of *Man is Man* (discussed in Chapter 2) the 'hero' is tricked, not only into selling a make-believe elephant, but also his name and role. What is being sold is false, both in the case of the elephant and in the case of the role. The formal innovation here is to switch narrative levels by making one part of the dramatic spectacle comment on another, each demonstrating that if something is reified, then something human has been responsible. It is through such play with form that the objects lose their opacity and become transparent, that the actor/spectator gets through the frozen concrete and discovers the abstract connection. The abstract is the socio-economic force which determines the object: the more one understands the abstract, the more one begins to be dissatisfied.

Lukács, on the other hand, wants to see real contradictions emerging from a single unified narrative, but this has to be done without betraying the hand of the artist. For him the task of the realist writer is twofold:

> first, the deliberate uncovering and artistic shaping of these connections, and second, but inseparably from the former, the artistic covering up of the connections achieved by the work of abstraction, the sublation of abstraction. Through this twofold labour a newly formed mediated immediacy of life comes into being, which, although it allows the essence to shine through at every moment (which cannot be the case with the immediacy of life), nevertheless appears as immediacy, as the surface of life, and what is more, as the whole surface of life in all its essential determinants – and not merely as a subjectively perceived and abstractly intensified moment isolated from the context of this totality. (Lukács, 1969, pp. 69–70)

This is the crux of Lukács's dispute with Brecht's work. Lukács ignores the fact that the techniques of documentation and montage also constitute a form of ordering in that they deliberately go beyond the bounds of realistic presentation. In particular, he refuses to grant Brecht's estrangement effect any epistemological status and accuses him of indulging in pure formalism. Yet paradoxically both Brecht and Lukács start out from the same position: nothing is immediately given; appearance is not objective reality. Immediate experience does not enable one to grasp historical contradictions, does not automatically yield to a view of appearances as historically constituted and hence transformable. Where they differ sharply is in their view of how this transformation is to be brought about. For Lukács, the great realist author, writing in an emancipatory historical moment, has intuitively provided a model for the future by embodying in his work the necessary transcendence of the contradictions. In opposition to this view Brecht turns the charge of formalism back on him for holding on to the traditional forms of writing when what is being represented in the contemporary world has markedly changed (*GW* 19, pp. 330–1). If the bourgeoisie is to be seen as bound to the fetishized forms of society, unable to see their historical determinants, whereas the proletariat has a better grasp of the total socio-economic and historical context, why tie the proletariat to an anachronistic form of representation? In any case, Brecht is not interested in a model which depends on an author harmonizing or transcending historical contradictions for a passive reader, but on creating an active reader who brings them to light:

> *Realistic* means: revealing the causal complex of society/unmasking the dominant perspective as the perspective of those in power/writing from the standpoint of the class which has available the most comprehensive solutions for the urgent problems with which human society is burdened/accentuating the moment of development/making possible the concrete, and abstraction from it.[5]

In order that the audience may abstract from its experience it has to be jolted out of its customary reverie. For Brecht the audience is an essential part of the work; the work is open and unfinished – unlike Lukács's organically constituted work – and calls on the productive capacities of the audience. Where Lukács wants the writer to show the world as potentially whole, hoping to inspire the revolutionary reader with utopian hope and faith, Brecht shows it as fragmented and infinitely transformable so as to force the audience into a continuous process of re-writing it.

The Brecht/Benjamin partnership

The association of Brecht and Benjamin arose out of their joint rejection of the traditional bourgeois autonomous work of art. Like Lukács, they looked to art for the founding of a new revolutionary consciousness which would transcend alienated social existence under capitalism, but, unlike Lukács, they vested their hope in a complete break with past modes of production. The ground of their alliance was their interest in the new processes of reproduction made possible by modern technologies and their belief in the radical effect these would have on the production and reception of art.

In the course of the 1930s Benjamin wrote a series of essays which show both explicitly and implicitly his debt to Brecht in providing him with material for a politically viable and historically adequate Marxist theory of culture. The essays in question are: 'What is Epic Theatre?' (two versions, 1931 and 1939); 'The Author as Producer' (1934); and 'The Work of Art in the Age of Mechanical Reproduction' (1936).[6] Since my aim here is not merely to give an account of Benjamin's contribution, but to outline how his quest for a materialist aesthetic found an answer in Brecht's praxis in the theatre, the essays are best discussed with a focus on specific issues rather than be confined within their own framework and chronology. The issues to the forefront are: the role of technology in the decline of autonomous art; the resultant transformation of the apparatus of production and of accustomed modes of perception; and the consequent call for a new political function for the arts, which will completely alter the relations between author, work, and audience. In short, the new technology is heralded as a means of freeing the means of production from the stranglehold of the capitalist state apparatus in order to make it available to socialist interests and purposes.

Benjamin and Brecht thought the opposite to Lukács with regard to avant-garde artistic techniques: they hoped with the help of these to break up the continuity of the historical world, and thus to undermine the supposed totality and reveal the contradictions under capitalism as a first step in the de-reification of modern mass urban life. According to Benjamin's seminal essay 'The Work of Art in the Age of Mechanical Reproduction', the new technology has altered our perception not only of art, but of all objects, in that the speed with which the new optical and acoustic apparatuses are able to capture and freeze images, enlarging them or slowing them down, disturbs our former passive and contemplative relationship to objects and forces us to take up an active and critical position towards them. Before the age of technology and mass-reproduction our perception of objects was determined by our response to their 'aura', the stored human associations which emanate from these objects towards the onlooker, drawing him into their orbit and enveloping him in an act of passive contemplation. In the age of mechanical reproduction this aura is lost because

> the technique of reproduction detaches the reproduced object from the domain of tradition. By making many reproductions it substitutes a plurality of copies for a unique existence. And in permitting the reproduction to meet the beholder or listener

in his own particular situation, it reactivates the object reproduced. (Benjamin, 1936, p. 223)

This alters our perception of it, for the object no longer gazes back at us reassuringly: 'a different nature opens itself to the camera than opens to the naked eye – if only because an unconsciously penetrated space is substituted for a space consciously explored by man' (1936, pp. 238–9). The object is no longer invested with the full authority of past cultural enactments, whether these have their basis in religious ritual or in the 'secular cult of beauty', which 'clearly showed that ritualistic basis in its decline'. It is the latter 'negative theology' that manifests itself in aestheticism, 'the doctrine of *l'art pour l'art*', which Benjamin sees as autonomous art's last stronghold, denying it all social function (1936, p. 226). It is clear that the concept of art as an 'auratic' object can be seen in terms of a kind of collective transference of the artist to his medium and a transference to that transference (what psycho-analysts call countertransference) on the part of the viewer to the work.[7] The concept of 'aura' is clearly an ideological one, although Benjamin does not spell this out very forcefully, at least not forcefully enough to satisfy Brecht, who comments on it in a much cited entry in his work-journal:

> he says: when you feel a gaze directed at you, even behind your back, you return it (!). the expectation that what you look at looks at you in return produces the aura. the latter is supposed to be in decline in recent times, along with the cultic. b[enjamin] has discovered this by means of an analysis of film, where the aura disintegrates through the reproducibility of works of art. pure mysticism, in a posture against mysticism. this is the form in which the materialist conception of history is adapted! it is fairly horrendous.[8]

Brecht has noticed that Benjamin is not entirely consistent in his attitude towards auratic art, although in the essay under discussion Benjamin welcomes its departure. He does not clearly define it as a species of commodity fetishism, as other critics have (see Solomon, 1979, pp. 545–6), nor expound on the imaginary dimension of the experience of viewer and object locked in a mirror-structure of gazes.[9]

However ambivalently Benjamin may feel towards traditional auratic art, he is fully aware that it has long since failed to serve any useful communal purpose. Rather there is the danger that the aestheticizing of the art object will render it useful for reactionary politics, such as fascism, which readily avails itself of the collective factor in order to exploit the aesthetics of war, to which 'communism responds by politicizing art' (Benjamin, 1936, p. 244). Art needs to be redeemed from the cult of the beautiful, and the age of mechanical reproduction marks the occasion for such a redemption. Benjamin looks in particular to the arts of photography and the cinema for offering the means of disturbing and disrupting the viewer's placid contemplation. First, the infinite reproducibility of the image would destroy any sense of uniqueness or authenticity; second, the technique of montage would ensure that the viewer was exposed to shocks of discontinuity, which would involve him in the process of construction and production; third, the new media were not just instruments for a different perception, but a means of critically examining perception and its contents, particularly collective perception. Benjamin realized that the new technical media through their capacity for registering the minute would reveal traces of experience hitherto inaccessible, uncovering what has not been seen before. In this he saw the connection to Freud:

> The film has enriched our field of perception with methods which can be illustrated by those of Freudian theory. Fifty years ago, a slip of the tongue passed more or less unnoticed. Only exceptionally may such a slip have revealed dimensions of depth in a conversation which had seemed to be taking its course on the surface. Since the *Psychopathology of Everyday Life* things have changed. This book isolated and made analysable things which had heretofore floated along unnoticed in the broad stream of perception. For the entire spectrum of optical, and now also acoustical, perception the film has brought about a similar deepening of apperception. (Benjamin, 1936, p. 237)

Hence Benjamin saw that the signs made visible by the new technical media had relevance for all kinds of sign-systems and were not merely confined to artistic ones: 'The camera introduces us to unconscious optics as does psychoanalysis to unconscious impulses' (1936, p. 239).

It has to be said, however, that Benjamin, for all his insight into the potential of the new media, misjudged their effect in that he believed that the mechanisms he described so brilliantly would automatically produce the desired politically progressive effect, for he did not, or would not foresee, as Adorno did, that they would lend themselves to commodification in turn. Although he foresaw the cult of the cinematic star, he thought that the elimination of the unique presence of the actor on the stage and the discontinuity of montage would curtail the charismatic effect of the actor on the audience; that is to say, he saw the revolutionary impact of the new media as inherent in the technical process and took for granted that a change in the relations of production would follow. But even though the means of production offered by the new media may call for a change in the old tired theatrical effects, they can also furnish a means of fostering bourgeois culture via the new methods of mass-production.

It is already clear that Brecht's epic theatre offered an exact model for Benjamin's concept of a new revolutionary apparatus of artistic production. In his essay 'The Author as Producer', Benjamin argues that a Brechtian *Umfunktionierung*, 'the transformation of forms and instruments of production', is the only way in which a politically committed art could engage with the class struggle, whereby a progressive writer might place himself on the side of the proletariat (Benjamin, 1934, p. 93). The hope was that in this joint enterprise the distinction between author and public, 'which the bourgeois press maintains by artificial means', would steadily narrow:

> The reader is always prepared to become a writer in the sense of being one who describes or prescribes. . . . Authority to write is no longer founded in a specialist training but in a poly-technical one, and so becomes common property. (Benjamin, 1934, p. 90)

This, however, entails the transformation of the bourgeois press, with its tendency merely to report or inform, into one which actively intervenes and mobilizes popular participation (Benjamin cites the Soviet writer and journalist Sergei Tretyakov). In Brecht's theatre Benjamin sees an obvious rhetorical parallel.

What interests him is that epic theatre is specifically concerned with the problems of aesthetic reception, and that it makes use of every possible modern technological device in order to break the hypnotic spell that the traditional theatre of illusion exerted over the spectator. It constantly points to the conditions of its own production by breaking up the dramatic action via songs, film strips, and captions, in order to interrupt the audience's customary field of perception, its tendency to take art for life:

Epic theatre . . . incessantly derives a lively and productive consciousness from the fact that it is theatre. This consciousness enables it to treat elements of reality as though it was setting up an experiment, with the 'conditions' at the end of the experiment, not at the beginning. They are not brought closer to the spectator, but distanced from him. When he recognizes them as real conditions it is not, as in naturalistic theatre, with complacency, but with astonishment. (Benjamin, 1931, p. 4)

Like Brecht, Benjamin sees the exploitation of the random effects of the new technical media as a way of turning the theatre into a laboratory, thereby separating literary and aesthetic forms from their ideological usage within the current relations of production and making them serve more progressive purposes: 'Epic theatre addresses itself to interested parties "who do not think unless they have a reason to"' (Benjamin, 1939, p. 16).

Benjamin is right to stress that it was part of Brecht's political purpose to enlist the audience as experts rather than as absorbers of culture, but he tends to underrate the importance Brecht assigned to pleasure. He also rules out too categorically the place of the emotions in the Brechtian aesthetic in maintaining that 'practically no appeal is made to the spectator's capacity for empathy' (1939, p. 18), forgetting that the V-effect operates dialectically, catching the audience out in their moments of emotional investment. Without involving the audience in contradictory feelings it would hardly be possible to galvanize them into any kind of productive thinking. In order to experience the contradictions of bourgeois production and reception some mode has to be found of making salient the limiting structures which have governed subjectivities so far.

Adorno against Brecht

Adorno's attack on 'committed' art is in opposition to Benjamin's desire for a politicized art of the modern and hence against his adoption of Brechtian theatre as a model for this kind of art. Nevertheless all three thinkers go beyond Lukács in their striving for de-reification in that they consider not only the production of the work of art but also the effects of its reception. But whereas both Brecht and Benjamin believed that the work of art would be revolutionized by technology and saw the transformation of techniques as a means of finishing with traditional bourgeois aesthetics,

Adorno thought otherwise. He objects to 'a sublimated remnant of certain Brechtian motifs' in Benjamin's (1936) essay, whereby Benjamin assigns a 'counter-revolutionary function' to the avant-garde autonomous work of art, and maintains that

> the principle that governs autonomous works of art is not the totality of their effects but their own inherent structure. They are knowledge as non-conceptual objects. This is the source of their nobility. It is not something of which they have to persuade men, because it has been given into their hands. . . . The notion of a 'message' in art, even when politically radical, already contains an accommodation to the world. (Adorno, 1980, p. 193)

By autonomous art Adorno does not mean the bourgeois aestheticization of art, quite the contrary. He readily agrees with Benjamin that the auratic element of the work of art is declining, but sees this not as a consequence of machine production but as a process immanent to the work itself whereby it resists appropriation by any particular ideology. For Adorno, autonomous art is precisely *not* art in the service of a prevailing power structure. Far from being counter-revolutionary, its magical element, which both Benjamin and Brecht object to, is in a dialectical relation with a certain freedom in which the work reveals a self-reflexive understanding of its own production process. This, its most progressive element, would become mere use-value if it were to be refunctioned in Brecht's political sense. For to politicize it, turning it into 'committed art', merely destroys its built-in resistance to commodification.

Adorno makes a distinction between the techniques of mechanical reproduction and technicality inherent in modern art itself. It is not technology which has put an end to traditional art, but modern art's own immanent relinquishing of auratic qualities. Adorno believes that Schönberg's atonal music provides a paradigm of a genuinely modern art: it not only resists commodification, but points self-reflexively towards its own contradictory strategies of evasion, articulating its resistance in its very technique of composition.[10] In an article which makes the attempt to read 'Adorno in Reverse', Andreas Huyssen turns Adorno's strategy of showing how easily modern art is corrupted by popular culture back on himself by arguing that Adorno can retrospectively be seen to explore 'how modernism itself appropriates and transforms elements of popular culture' (Huyssen, 1983, p. 13). As an example he cites Adorno's (1952) criticism of Richard Wagner's music, in which Adorno regards Wagner as a kind of precursor to Schönberg: 'All of modern music has developed in resistance to his [Wagner's] predominance – and yet all of its elements are latently present in him' (Adorno, 1971, p. 504). Although Adorno's essay is ostensibly an account of the 'birth of fascism out of the spirit of the *Gesamtkunstwerk*' (German romanticism's concept of an art which obeyed its own laws and transgressed all previous categories of composition), his study can also be read as an account of the origin of commodification in nineteenth-century high art (Huyssen, 1983, p. 29). The phantasmagoria of Wagner's operas have veiled all traces of labour that went into their production, yet his music yields to the pressure of the commodity form in producing its dream world in the form of illusion and myth: the false totality of the music is shown up by the way it disintegrates into popular passages in the course of its reception. Commodification is therefore not only the result of external forces but is already nascent in art which tries to free itself from its traditional form, ready for external forces to seize on it:

> Adopting Benjamin's designation of the traditional work of art by the concept of aura, the presence of that which is not present, the culture industry is defined by the fact that is does not strictly counterpose another principle to that of aura, but rather that it conveys the decaying aura as a foggy mist. By this means the culture industry betrays its own abuses. (Adorno, 1975, p. 13)

For Adorno, Schönberg's music plays out a resistance to any kind of perverted use-value by contradicting itself dialectically from within, where a non-autonomous work will artfully collude with the masses to sell itself. The genuinely modern work has a quality of play that cannot be appropriated; it slips away from any direct form of representation. It is this quality Adorno also finds in the works of Kafka and Beckett, functioning as a negation of what he sees as a totally 'administered world'.

Adorno was implacably opposed to mass culture, though not merely because of elitist tastes of his own (Jay, 1984, p. 119). Together with Max Horkheimer he coined the term 'culture industry' to designate the domination of the masses from the enlightenment onwards by means of an ever-increasing technical rationality:

> To speak of culture was always contrary to culture. Culture as a common denominator already contains in embryo that

schematization and process of cataloguing and classification which bring culture within the sphere of administration. And it is precisely the industrialized, the consequent subsumption which entirely accords with this notion of culture. By subordinating in the same way and to the same end all areas of intellectual creation, by occupying men's senses from the time they leave the factory in the evening to the time they clock in again the next morning with matter that bears the impress of the labour process that they themselves have to sustain throughout the day, this subsumption mockingly satisfies the concept of a unified culture which the philosophers of personality contrasted with mass culture. (Horkheimer and Adorno, 1973, p. 131)

The culture industry, while promising fulfilment and emancipation, will in reality prevent the development of any genuine mass culture from taking shape. In this he was influenced by three elements in his own experience: mass culture in the Weimar era, the fascist glorification of folk culture, and popular culture in the United States after his emigration (see Huyssen, 1975, p. 4). He feared the ever-expanding rationale of technical advancement and its effect on both individual and collective freedom. Like Lukács he deeply distrusted certain versions of modernism and judged that both Brecht and Benjamin were overstating the progressive potential of mass art. He attacked what he believed to be mere experimentation:

Formal structures which challenge the lying positivism of meaning can easily slide into a different kind of vacuity, positivistic arrangements, empty jugglings with elements. They fall within the very sphere from which they seek to escape. The extreme is literature which undialectically confuses itself with science and vainly tries to fuse with cybernetics. (Adorno, in Anderson *et al.*, 1980, p. 191)

Adorno not only criticizes Brecht for what he considers to be tendentious content, such as the glorification of the Party (*The Mother, The Measures Taken*), or his populist strain, whereby he reduces fascism to 'a trivial gangster organization' in *The Resistible Rise of Arturo Ui* (Adorno, 1980, pp. 182 and 183). He also accuses him of practising an empty formalism: 'The primacy of lesson over pure form, which Brecht intended to achieve, became a formal device itself. . . . The substance of Brecht's artistic work was the didactic play as an artistic principle' (Adorno, 1980, p. 185).

Hence, he implies, Brecht's formalism is tainted in being forced to subserve the ideology of his anti-capitalist politics: 'the homeliness and simplicity of his tone is thus a fiction. It betrays itself both by signs of exaggeration and by stylized regression to archaic or provincial forms of expression' (Adorno, 1980, p. 185). Adorno thus condemns Brecht on all counts: for his attempt to turn the theatre into a laboratory; for his espousal of a version of socialism Adorno judged to be totalitarian ('when Brecht became a panegyrist of its harmony, his lyric voice had to swallow chalk, and it started to grate' (1980, p. 185)); and, most of all, for what he sees as a reduction of the aesthetic to the political, whatever its content may be. He accuses Brecht of conjuring away 'the true horror of fascism' (1980, p. 184), without considering that Brecht's object might not be so much parody, but a desire to show fascism to be a continuation of Weimar bourgeois democracy. In this view the imitation of an elevated style (in the scene where Ui is educated into leadership speech) is significant as a consciously acquired rhetoric and theatricalization of bourgeois speech which betrays its perverted use-value for fascism. This is no mock-heroic style in the spirit that Büchner uses it in his drama *Danton's Tod* in order to parody Weimar classicism. The aim is rather to point to a general aesthetizing of politics via German fascism, and to show how this fulfilled the subjective needs of the petty bourgeoisie (see Knopf, 1980, pp. 232–4). What Adorno failed to see in objecting to this corruption of the aesthetic by the political was a certain dialectical element, namely that Brecht was deconstructing the perverse strategies performed by fascism in its appropriation and exaggeration of bourgeois rhetoric for gangsters and fascists in the attempt to divert attention from political reality. 'The didactic play as artistic principle' is not just mere propaganda: what is at stake is not mere 'defamiliarization' but 'distanciation' (a favoured recent translation of *Verfremdung*), the form betraying the split consciousness which still inhabits it, thereby encouraging the audience (hopelessly unequal to any such task in Adorno's pessimistic assessment) to engage in the production of that particular mode of thinking Brecht called 'interventionist' (*GW* 18, p. 237), which questions things and events with regard to the possibility of change and transformation.

The logic of the argument against Brecht in Adorno's 'Commitment' essay is byzantine in the extreme. For intermingled with his arraignments is the admission that it is foolish to try and save Brecht for the West by distinguishing the artist from the politician, 'futile to separate the beauties, real or imaginary, of his works from their political intentions. The task of immanent criticism, which alone is dialectical, is rather to synthesize assessment of the validity of his forms with that of his politics' (Adorno, 1980, p. 186). Adorno cannot prevent himself, even when he is grudgingly giving Brecht his due, from seeing him as a 'transcendent' rather than an 'immanent' critic: whereas the immanent critic is prepared to live with dialectical change, the transcendent critic falsely assumes a godlike detachment from the ideological process, an objectivity rigid and positivistic, representative of an oppressive system. A successful work bears evidence of inner contradictions, refusing to deny the dialectical strain. Any object/person thus becomes subject to a 'heightened perception' that eschews reification, either of object or person, and it is only this approach which works against the official manipulation of 'popular' culture (Adorno, 1967, pp. 31–4).

This position will necessarily refute any concerted attempt at a politicization of the arts, such as the one undertaken by Brecht and Benjamin; similarly it will set itself against any notion of a reflection theory, such as the one propounded by Lukács, which assumes a ready-made totality before perception takes place. Only the autonomous work of high modernism, pure and uncorrrupted by any professed social aspiration, can negate the false and by this means hope to achieve a transformation of the subject.

For Adorno, then, the subject persists despite reification, but his notion of the subject is still tied to traditional subject philosophy and the stable self of the bourgeois age. The great problem is, as all his critics, for or against him, point out, that he has no notion how a change of consciousness might lead to a change in social conditions, how intellectual praxis related to social praxis. As Susan Buck-Morss points out in her lucid study, 'he viewed critical negativity as a creative force in itself, believed that it could, through its own strength, at least attain knowledge of the truth' (1977, p. 36). For Adorno any resistance to reification can only be discerned in certain privileged forms of art, and this position maintains the notion of the artist as a special kind of high priest, innocent of any sort of didactic purpose.

Towards a revolutionary art

The relation of art to the prevailing power structure is central to the notion of crisis in modernity, both to the crisis initiated by the historical avant-garde and to its continuation in the present modernism/postmodernism debate (dealt with in Chapter 5). Whereas art had once fulfilled a cultic function via an aesthetics of the beautiful – thereby serving to reinforce the collective aspirations of society – with the coming of age of bourgeois capitalism this function had undergone a sea-change: whilst still assuming to represent universal values, art was now serving the interests of a privileged group. Yet, although both modernism and the avant-garde were intent on challenging traditional forms of art, they did not pursue the same revolutionary aims. The challenge to representation was politicized only in the latter movement: the historical avant-garde explicitly set their hope in art's ceasing to be a cult object and becoming part of a general revolutionary praxis. For them a politicized form of art must involve a radical change of form in order to escape reification.

Of the four protagonists under discussion three aligned themselves with this view. The dissenting voice was Lukács, who insisted that the foundation for a revolutionary consciousness resided in continuing with what remained of the progressive line of bourgeois literature in its most emancipatory moments: he cherished the hope that readers would perceive the mismatch of their lived impoverished experience with the experience of totality embedded in the great work of art, and would feel collectively impelled to take up the fight for change. Unlike Adorno, who applauded avant-gardist techniques (while rejecting the technology), Lukács deeply distrusted modernism's drive towards discontinuity and rupture as detrimental to any utopian vision.

Adorno, on the other hand, was convinced that art's utopian aspirations were under threat from mass culture and needed guarding from the administered world. Hence, he too wished to save the autonomy of art but by different means and for different reasons: he believed, paradoxically, that as soon as art becomes politicized, it ceases to be revolutionary, for it will then either be implicated in the petrified relations of the old culture or become prey to those of the new one. Its only hope of resistance was to close itself off from general consumption and remain autonomous. Although Adorno was concerned to further individual reception of works of art by kindred spirits able to tune in to the contradictions immanent in high modernist art, unlike Brecht and Benjamin he had no room in his theory of production for any general aesthetics of reception.

The partnership of Brecht and Benjamin arose out of their joint rejection of the traditional autonomous work of art, with its way of sucking in the contemplative viewer. They were the first to make a move in a new direction. For Benjamin, Brecht's epic theatre pointed towards a new theory of production, whereby the scientific uses of art offered by the modernization of technology would replace the lure of an auratic art. They both believed that the new techniques could be used to change the function of art, revealing the political in the cultic, and giving the reader/viewer a productive role and a chance of intervening in the class conflict. The destruction of the aura meant that past political experience could now be made available: the new technical apparatus could discover hitherto undivined traces of past social experience. The new techniques would work towards the destruction of continuous experience (*Erfahrung*) and emphasize the discontinuous (*Erlebnis*) (Benjamin, 1982, pp. 180–5). The new media would not only serve as instruments for a heightened perception, but also as a means of critically examining that very perception, revealing another sign system, hitherto unnoticed, showing traces of the compulsiveness of existence, and also registering past communal experience. Both of these, negative and positive, might be harnessed to the new revolutionary purpose. For here a new production apparatus seemed to offer itself as means of breaking the hold of the institution on the forces of production.

Brecht and Benjamin were *theoretically* right in believing that the new technology would radically alter the production and reception of art, but they were over-optimistic in hoping for the desired political effect. The relations between work and audience did not change in the way they foresaw. It was Adorno and Lukács who proved to be *historically* right: technology increased rather than decreased art's vulnerability to commodification. Technology turned culture into kitsch even more than Adorno could have anticipated: the gap between the elitist and the popular widened until both sides were reified in their political positions. The relations of production (Adorno's 'culture industry') managed to depoliticize and pervert the relation of the masses to technology and undo all the radical potential of the changes brought about by the new technology. Brecht and Benjamin were wrong to think that there was something in the form itself which would deliver liberalization. But the fact that they were historically wrong does not mean that the new rhetoric made available cannot be used for different ends: they are not wrong theoretically, because (as Chapter 5 will show) it is at least arguable that it is still possible to resist mass culture. The question whether technology increases or decreases art's vulnerability to commodification can only be answered historically.

Brecht does not merely stay with the glorification of technology. He always tries to place the spectator square within the relations of production. For him capitalism is a prime example of the excessive alienation of the subject from the relations of production. His theatre aims to show that between the outward objectification of the subject and its inner experience there is a split, which will become critical in the capitalist world. The subject is encouraged to think of its individuality as independent of capitalist relations, and is therefore unable to see its own objectivity. Both objects and subjects are represented as given and it is this which leads to reification.

Brecht's epic theatre tries to foster an understanding of such contradictions (*Erkenntnis der Widersprüche*), using the new means of production to call for a change in the old theatrical effects, yet finding that they can also be the means of fostering bourgeois ideologies. Brecht knew as well as Adorno that the materials with which he worked were contaminated by those who owned the means of production, but he never ceased to try ways of dialectically transforming them in the effort to turn them from capitalist tools into tools for human emancipation.

Whether the political potential of avant-garde techniques is exhausted, whether postmodernism can refunction the political in radical modernism, is the subject of further debate. Postmodern theatre, as will be seen, pursues the importance of actuality in the theatre. Technical mediation actualizes the work in a different way from that advocated by Brecht and Benjamin: 'the material is used not to signify but to present; it signals more than it signifies' (Pontbriand, 1982, p. 157). The radically fragmented form of the text, the breaking of the theatrical codes, has resulted in the phenomenon called 'performance' (see Chapter 6), a theatre of shocks calling upon a new kind of spectator.

Notes

1 See also Russell (1985), who upholds the distinction between 'the different, if historically parallel, traditions of the avant-garde and modernism' (p. 7), and Lunn (1985), who supplies a detailed historical survey of the modernist revolt in its relation to capitalist economy, society, and culture, as filtered through the critical thought of Lukács, Brecht, Benjamin, and Adorno.

2 See Gallas (1972), pp. 124–41 and pp. 148–63, who gives a lucid and amply documented account of the controversies surrounding the proletarian revolutionary writers, on which my discussion of Lukács draws.

3 For a political account of this aesthetic debate contrary to that of Lukács, see Berman (1977).

4 See Berman, 1977, p. 173, who points out that there is an inconsistency here in, on the one hand, calling upon an author to use the 'science of Marxism-Leninism' – a philosophical explanation of the human world which uses science for its credentials – and on the other hand, claiming that art is not part of science.

5

> *Realistisch* heisst: den gesellschaftlichen Kausalkomplex aufdecken / die herrschenden Gesichtspunkte als die Gesichtspunkte der Herrschenden entlarvend / vom Standpunkt der Klasse aus schreibend welche für die dringendsten Schwierigkeiten, in denen die menschliche Gesellschaft steckt, die breitesten Lösungen bereit hält / das Moment der Entwicklung betonend / konkret und das Abstrahieren ermöglichend. (*GW* 19, p. 326)

6 For the essays of 1931, 1934, and 1939, see Benjamin (1973), and for the essay of 1936, see Benjamin (1982); details in bibliography.

7 For a brief elaboration on the ideological implications of regarding art as a highly invested cultural object, see Wright (1984), pp. 96–7.

8

> er sagt: wenn man einen blick auf sich gerichtet fühlt, auch im rücken, erwidert man ihn (!). die erwartung, dass, was man anblickt, einen selber anblickt, verschafft die aura. diese soll in letzter zeit im zerfall sein, zusammen mit dem kultischen. b[enjamin] hat das bei der analyse des films entdeckt, wo aura zerfällt durch die reproduzierbarkeit von kunstwerken. alles mystik, bei einer haltung gegen mystik. in solcher form wird die materialistische geschichtsauffassung adaptiert! es ist ziemlich grauenhaft. (*Arbeitsjournal*, p. 14)

9 See Eagleton (1981), pp. 37–9, for an illuminating comparison with Lacan's dialectic of the eye and the gaze.

10 For a more detailed discussion on this point, see Lunn (1985), pp. 262–4.

5

Brecht and postmodernism:
theatricalizing the unpresentable

So far Brecht has been regarded in a modernist context, as an innovator and promoter of aesthetic contradictions with a firm belief in the political and ideological function of art as a means of producing a collective subject. It now remains to be seen whether this context exhausts Brecht's potential as a dramatist and critical thinker, as is implied by those modernists and postmodernists who have retired Brecht, considering him harmless and ineffectual (Hofmann, 1980, and Handke, 1968, p. 7). In this chapter I want to turn the early Brecht, the Brecht without the *Fabel*, generally still taken as the anarchistic, nihilistic, undisciplined, phase-one Brecht (see Chapter 1), into a postmodernist Brecht whose effects can be felt almost anywhere in the theatre except in the staging of his own plays.

In order to clear a space both for the early plays and for the post-Brechtian theatre to be introduced in the next chapter, I need to discuss some versions of postmodernism. In the course of this discussion and of the examples of Brecht's practice that follow I shall hope to dispense with the notion of a three-phase Brecht, maintaining instead with Heiner Müller that there are many Brechts (Müller, 1986, p. 33). I would like to distinguish an unfamiliar postmodernist Brecht from a familiar modernist one, that is to say, the didactic Brecht of the *Fabel* of dialectical contradiction as against the early de-centred Brecht of the *Fabel* of self-deconstruction. He seems to make a good pivot for reviewing the current postmodernist debate. The tension between the Brechts might even be viewed in terms of a modernist Habermas–Brecht (celebrated and scorned as a classic) and a postmodernist Lyotard–Brecht (hailed as a *sine qua non* of any future developments in the theatre).

The postmodernist debate

The debate on modernity outlined in Chapter 4 is relevant to the discussion on postmodernism. It demonstrates how literary and artistic modernism is faced with a particular problem when technological progress results in the development of media. The fact that technology has erased some of the distinctions between 'high' and 'low' art is seen as positive and constructive by some (Brecht, Benjamin, and now Habermas), and negative or problematic by others (Lukács, Adorno, and now Jameson and Eagleton). The assumptions of those against are predicated on the belief that 'high' art in its avant-garde form breeds useful contradictions, whereas 'low' or 'popular' art colludes with capitalism. Where in the course of the modernist debate Brecht and Benjamin tried to subvert the autonomy of art, Lukács and Adorno tried, although in different ways, to preserve it. In the current debate the stakes are somewhat different, even though there still remains the question of the effects of mass culture. Postmodernism has issued a challenge to modernism for its unrelenting hostility to mass culture (for a full critical account, see Huyssen, 1984).

Jürgen Habermas

Habermas (Adorno's assistant from 1956) has a more positive view of mass culture than his predecessors of the Frankfurt School. He came to see Adorno's refusal to countenance mass art as a 'strategy of hibernation' (Habermas, 1979, p. 43), coming to the same conclusion as Brecht and Benjamin, albeit by another route. Habermas has a certain faith in the value of a collective mode of reception in that he sees the changing patterns of the mass media and the birth of a new mass audience as a way of breaking up the old class structures (see Habermas, 1985c). In placing some hope in a collective mode of reception he revises Adorno and Horkheimer's unhistorical conception of a culture industry and gives it a specific historical context. Following Max Weber, he argues that, with the falling apart of unified views of the world, culture has split up into the three autonomous realms of science, morality, and art, 'structures of cognitive-instrumental, of moral practical and of aesthetic-expressive rationality', all of which require specialist handling (1985a, p. 9). Habermas sees the three-way split not simply as a disaster, but as a chance for art to become re-integrated into the life-world, thereby relinquishing that modernist autonomy Adorno had uncompromisingly demanded. Habermas believes that the split into separate spheres of knowledge cannot and should not be reversed, but dialectically advanced. The hoped-for aim is that art, now placed in the sphere of 'aesthetic-practical rationality', might become part of everyday communicative practice, while paradoxically – or contradictorily – retaining a special function. That function, however, is not so very different from that which the historical avant-garde assigned to art, and indeed Habermas sees it as a kind of continuation and aligns himself with the historical avant-garde's 'transformation of aesthetic experience . . . in the direction of the decentring and unbounding of subjectivity', a decentring which 'indicates an increased sensitivity to what remains unassimilated in the interpretive achievements of pragmatic, epistemic, and moral mastery of the demands and challenges of everyday situations; it effects an openness to the expurgated elements of the unconscious, the fantastic, and the mad, the material and the bodily' (Habermas, 1985b, p. 201).

While in one sense one wants to applaud Habermas for including such phenomena within the category of aesthetic-practical rationality – a category in the spirit of Brecht – one is suspicious that the price of art as everyday communicative practice and as filter for repressed communal elements of experience and utopian hope might be the abandonment of its will to challenge the existing authority. Although such a projected harmony might produce the hope of a reconciliation between freedom and authority, the 'balanced and undistorted intersubjectivity of everyday life' (Habermas, 1985b, p. 202), this hope must be distinguished from the unconscious ideology of a repressive system. Indeed it was this difficulty which led Adorno to reject the social *tout court*. Furthermore, Habermas's account of the social application of art lacks a theory of the precise mode of its integration into his blueprint for a rational society. And that was also Brecht's problem. What is clear is that he continues to uphold the aesthetic principles of modernism against an emerging postmodernist aesthetic, which he rightly sees as much a question of politics as a matter of style (see Huyssen, 1984, p. 36). In either case he envisages the possibility of incorporating avant-garde aesthetics into his project of modernity and meanwhile charges those he sees as representing postmodernism in France, a line which for him 'leads from Georges Bataille via Michel Foucault to Jacques Derrida', with the designation of 'young conservatives', who 'recapitulate the basic experience of aesthetic modernity', who 'claim as their own the revelations of a decentred subjectivity, emancipated from the imperatives of work and usefulness' (Habermas, 1985a, p. 14).

Fredric Jameson and Terry Eagleton

Can modernism be seen as dialectically continued in postmodernism or is there a break? As if following on from Adorno's pessimistic view that kitsch 'suffocates' culture, Fredric Jameson argues that postmodernism not only emerges as a reaction against specific forms of high modernism, but, to add insult to injury, it 'incorporates' kitsch in such a way that high and low are fused. It does this by means of pastiche, rather than by parodic 'quotation', as modernists like Joyce or Mahler might have done, who by way of a sympathetic or malicious parody were able to revitalize their target and thereby grant it some kind of authentic existence (Jameson, 1985, pp. 112–14). What we are now left with, according to Jameson, is a highly commodified art, which has lost all sense of its own history and reveals itself as a symptom of late consumer capitalism, there being 'very little in either the form or the content of contemporary art that contemporary society finds intolerable or scandalous', for advertising is 'fed by postmodernism in all the arts and inconceivable without it' (1985, p. 125). Hence for Jameson postmodernism not only lacks the critical potential of high modernism, but serves to reinforce 'the logic of consumer capitalism' (*ibid.*). He is therefore in agreement with Habermas as regards a positive view of the modernism that was and a negative one of the postmodernism that is, though his case is neither bound up with a reformed notion of the Enlightenment spirit nor with a belief in the continuing critical power of modernism in any general way (see Jameson, 1984, pp. 58–9).

Terry Eagleton, in response to Jameson, also proclaims a lack of enthusiasm for postmodernism, but he has a different set of reservations. Postmodernism, he maintains, *does* go in for a form of parody, and what it mimes and parodies is 'the formal resolution of art and social life attempted by the avant-garde, while remorsely emptying it of its political content'. It presents us with 'a grisly parody of socialist utopia', and thereby alienates us from our own alienation, persuading us 'to recognize that utopia not as some remote *telos*, but, amazingly, as nothing less than the present itself' (Eagleton, 1985, p. 61). Modernist art, however, is equally doomed, for in trying to resist becoming an object of commodity culture, instantly exchangeable, it ends up being used as a commodity fetish, 'its solution to reification part of that very problem' (p. 67). Modernist art takes on an illusory value through the very remoteness and uniqueness for which it strives and thereby acquires an individualistic bourgeois cast. What Eagleton finally asks for is an art in which the contradictions of modernism are made explicitly political: that is to say, the separateness of subjectivity can be made political, but modernism never did this because it failed to analyse why the splitting-off had occurred. Eagleton wants a dialectical move which swerves away from the present drastic crossing of a commodified modernism with an institutionalized avant-garde via a 'transformed rationality', which unlike the version that Habermas has produced, at present remains undefined.

Jean-François Lyotard

A different position is taken by Lyotard, who believes that postmodernism has already made a dialectical move. The 'post' is not to be understood as a simple chronology, as a break with modernism. On the contrary, it is a moment of 'working through' (in the psychoanalytical sense) the texts of past modernists in an attempt to understand these anew:

> If we give up this responsibility, it is certain that we are condemned to repeat, without any displacement, the modern neurosis, the Western schizophrenia, paranoia and so on. This being granted, the 'post-' of postmodernity does not mean a process of coming back or flashing back, feeding back, but of *ana*-lysing, *ana*-mnesing, of reflecting. (Lyotard, 1986, p. 7)

For Lyotard, paradoxically, 'a work can become modern only if it is first postmodern' (1984, p. 79). This is because modernism is still in the grip of an 'aesthetic of the sublime', allowing 'the unpresentable', the non-epistemic, what cannot be epistemized, 'only to be put forward as the missing contents', as some kind of transcendental value, while continuing to offer the reader the solace of beautiful form. The postmodern, on the other hand, 'searches for new presentations, not in order to enjoy them but in order to impart a stronger sense of the unpresentable'. Like the philosopher, the postmodern artist does not work according to pre-established rules:

Those rules and categories are what the work of art itself is looking for. The artist and the writer, then, are working without rules in order to formulate the rules of what *will have been done*. Hence the fact that work and text have the character of an *event*; hence also, they always come too late for their author, or, what amounts to the same thing, their being put into work, their realization (*mise en oeuvre*) always begins too soon. (Lyotard, 1984, p. 81)

That is to say, the author is always behindhand with the interpretation of the text. The author finds that another, be it writer or critic, is realizing the text and producing the meaning he did not envisage or understand. Works not governed by pre-established rules always run the risk of being dubbed 'anarchistic', or 'nihilistic' (as the examples of early Brecht will bear out; note also his many attempts to revise and re-view his own works, in an attempt to forestall, to use Lyotard's formulation, 'what will have been done').

In Lyotard's reading of Kant 'the sublime emerges when there is no longer a beautiful form', when we witness the emergence of something monstrous and formless, the moment of the imminence of death (1986, p. 11 and p. 10). For Lyotard this is also the moment when regulation and rules are in abeyance. Like Brecht, Lyotard is determined to reject any single unifying explanation of the world (particularly of justice) that is based on a fixed ontology. In the dialogues collected together under the title *Just Gaming* (Lyotard and Thébaud, 1985) he argues that, since there is no fundamental ontology, no transcendental support, it behoves one to discover the 'ruses' by which the constrictions of any traditional language game might be overcome.

For Lyotard consensus violates the heterogeneity of language games, and it is therefore not surprising to find him polemicizing against Habermas for wanting to save modernism from postmodernism in the hope of 'finishing' the modernist project and producing a unifying interdisciplinary discourse. His belief in heterogeneity makes him as suspicious of mass culture as he is of consensus, for he is conscious that the words 'popular' and 'democratic' have undergone a slippage of meaning. They are subsumed under the term 'pop', a product which produces its own commodified audience. Here, then, Lyotard to some extent joins forces with Jameson and Eagleton, but he parts from them in that he believes that resistance can be introduced into the cultural industry, 'a feeling of disturbance, in the hope that this disturbance will be followed by reflection . . . it's up to every artist to decide by what means s/he thinks s/he can produce this disturbance' (1986, p. 58).

The notion of resistance to any imposed reified meaning is central to the project of those who believe in the radical potential of postmodernism. This is not only resistance in an overt political sense, but resistance to any transference to the current power structure. Inevitably this involves problematizing the very activity of reference by playing on the inherently dialectical structure of perception, conscious against unconscious, eye against gaze, symbolic against imaginary. In postmodernist art everything is subject to a V-effect and so the concept becomes redundant. A perennial V-effect is the result of the mismatch between signifier and signified, the uncanniness of the concrete, which itself resists the attempt to name and define it.

Nevertheless, it is that very resistance to definition which undermines the collectivity of the audience and encourages the recognition of what is marginal in experience. Lyotard believes that the modern (and its retrospective continuation into postmodern) is characterized by an aesthetics of 'experimentation', whereby art explores the unsayable, sensed but as yet unperceived concrete, irrespective of whether there is a recognized subject who is already an appropriate receiver of the communication:

> What is at stake in artistic language today is experimentation. And to experiment means . . . that if the artefact produced is really strong, it will wind up producing its own readers, its own viewers, its own listeners. In other words, the experimental work will have as one of its effects the constitution of a pragmatic situation that did not exist before. It is the message itself, by its very form, that will elicit both the one who receives it and the one who sends it. They are able then to communicate with each other . . . sometimes this takes centuries, sometimes twenty years, sometimes three, and there are times when it happens right away. (Lyotard and Thébaud, 1985, p. 10)

Brecht

Brecht's early plays may be distinguished from the later ones and also from the *Lehrstücke* by being seen as an example of Lyotard's notion of 'experimentation' rather than as examples of his own view of an experimental 'theatre of the scientific age' in which he and his co-workers self-consciously probe history for its repression of the political facts of life. His newer, earlier 'experimentation' resides rather in probing the constitution of the subject at the intersection of social (historical) and psychological (transhistorical) forces. It is this project with its attendant critical examination of perception and its contents which qualifies for a reading of Brecht as a postmodernist.

The postmodernist Brecht is different from the modernist Brecht who produced the split subjects of the 'great' plays and who attributed this split to the divisive nature of bourgeois capitalism. In this other Brecht of the early plays the performative mode appears instead of the denotative mode of the later ones, with the result that accidental meaning subverts any didactic intention. To use Benjamin's terminology again, it is a case of '*Erlebnis* (experiencing the random shocks of life) taking the place of '*Erfahrung*' (experiencing life as a continuity).

Where in the 'great' plays the *Fabel* provided sense and meaning despite the disruptions of the epic mode, in the early plays theatricalization of experience undermines reference so that anything can happen in the communication process, both between one character and another, and between stage and audience. To theatricalize is to engage in a fictive experimenting with the interaction of language and experience, to explore the very ground of representation. According to Lyotard the language games one is nevertheless forced to play expose the players to dire risks as they pursue the satisfactions their subjectivities demand:

> The social bond, understood as a multiplicity of language games, very different among themselves, each with its own pragmatic efficacy and its capability of positioning people in precise places in order to have them play their parts, is traversed by terror, that is, by the fear of death. (Lyotard, 1986, p. 99)

In these plays there is no appeal to the audience to solve the contradictions outside the deliberately unfinished work. The work of the plays is on language, with the effect that the characters are not self-present but continually constitute themselves via an other. This other may include the individual subject, but the audience as such is not inscribed in the text. On the contrary, there is rather a move away from soliciting any kind of collective perception, a move which anticipates the examples of post-Brechtian theatre to be discussed in Chapter 6.

The aesthetics of early Brecht: *Baal* and *In the Jungle of the Cities*

He who wants to make a great leap, must be prepared to take a few steps back. Today sustains itself through yesterday into tomorrow.[1]

In the battle with the old the new ideas get their sharpest formulations.[2]

Brecht's early plays position the spectator differently from the later ones, and also differently from the *Lehrstücke*. These plays have certain features in common which might be seen as elements of negation. This is why they cannot so easily be reduced to a *Fabel*, although both Marxists and humanists have tried to appropriate them. Marxist critics see them as subjective, impressionistic, and self-indulgently aesthetic. Humanist critics fall back on biography (see Chapter 1, p. 6) and talk about the anarchistic tendencies due to the immaturity of Brecht in his early twenties. They like to cite Brecht's retrospective 1954 comment on *Baal*: 'I admit (and warn you) the play is lacking in wisdom' (*GW* 17, p. 948). Marxist critics cite other parts of the same critical fragment: 'The play *Baal* could present difficulties for those who have not learned to think dialectically. They are not likely to find anything in it apart from the glorification of a blatant egotism.'[3] Since Brecht himself was ambivalent and never satisfied with the results,[4] it is not hard to make out a case for either position.

I would like to concentrate on *Baal* and *In the Jungle of the Cities*, written by the young Brecht at the age of twenty and twenty-three respectively. In my discussion I am going to maintain that the power of the two plays resides not in their documentary effectiveness, but in their formal characteristics. As has been seen, their content can be appropriated one way or another, but if they have any political use-value it is perhaps more likely to be found in their formal properties than in any uniform conceptual view, such as vitalism, nihilism, anarchism, or even Marxism. Their politico-aesthetic function resides rather in the way Brecht manages to make the spasmodic, discontinuous perceptions of a reality-in-process into a theatrical object, thus challenging our automatic interpretations of the concrete and our assumptions that words are able to match that which we sensuously perceive. Most of all, the plays are an attack on our assumptions of stable identity, our own and that of others, for in these plays no one has a fixed identity,

98

least of all the 'hero', who tries to wrest it from others in a ceaseless round of aggressiveness and exploitation. *Baal* and *In the Jungle of the Cities* offer a challenge to representation in a different mode from that of the later plays of Brecht, which tend to be purged of the shocks to our mimetic understanding. The early plays do not yield a relatively ordered collage of happenings, conveniently subtitled in a way which foregrounds the *Fabel*, but are blatantly anti-narrative in form. Impossible to package for consumption, they disrupt normal modes of perception, merely pointing to happenings, postures, and processes. They cannot be reduced to any particular ideology, including those of Marxism or existentialism, because this would amount to an attempt to join up a deliberately decentred view of reality. Instead they expose the spectator to an onslaught on representation from within its very practice in an attempt to undermine existing discourses, which already embody in their structuring principles the ideological reproductions of the culture they serve. Brecht, as will be seen, is out to re-define our understandings of concrete limit-experiences, re-staging the dramas of birth, love, sickness, and death in the attempt to articulate alternative meanings. The plays provide a knowledge of the condition of representation for a subject (character and spectator) in such a way that s/he can only have access to such knowledge via a theatricalization of experience. The ultimate aim of my discussion of these plays will thus be to show how Brecht makes such experience into a theatrical object.

Baal

The form of the play is that of a series of highly fragmentary scenes which stage the subjectivity of a wild but educated poet,[5] who lives out his life by eating, drinking, reciting, singing in the grog houses and cafés of the day, procuring sexual encounters and staging them indiscriminately in his attic rooms and the surrounding streets, fields, and forests. Women only too readily make themselves into his sexual objects and he moves from one to the other, leaving a trail of corpses in his wake, including that of a male lover. He finally dies in the forest, unrepentant and abandoned by all.

Baal, Brecht argues, is 'asocial, but in an asocial society' (Schmidt, 1969), for here an 'I' confronts a world only able to recognize a productivity which can be exploited rather than one that can be utilized. It follows that Marxist critics can argue that Baal is an active anti-bourgeois, an anarchist only in a society which pays lip-service to individualism but cannot accept it when it appears in its extreme form (Knopf, 1980, p. 16). The asocial Baal exploits the exploited, putting the basic drives on show for all to see. Brecht writes to Caspar Neher, his old schoolfriend and life-long collaborator, in 1918: 'I am writing a comedy: Baal guzzles, Baal dances, Baal is transfigured! A hamster, a great sensualist, a clod who leaves greasespots in the sky, a crazy fellow with immortal intestines.'[6] The general argument is that the early Brecht wanted to affirm the subversive energy of the basic drives in the context of a bourgeois society which insisted on putting the reality principle before the pleasure principle. An undialectical interpretation would be that this drive-bound creature acts as a provocation to a society which demands that the drives be repressed and as a shock reminder of what this entails. This might be turned into a dialectical interpretation if one points out that Baal does not withdraw from society, but on the contrary, uses others, particularly women, in order to gratify his needs; his being 'asocial in an asocial society' is thus not wholly to be laid at society's door. Yet perverse sexuality becomes a positive act against bourgeois morality, a more revolutionary move than cravenly surrendering in the style of *The Private Tutor* and *Man is Man* (by committing acts of self-castration) in order to stay in the system. Brecht himself, though he held to the radical effects of the asocial, expressed misgivings about the political effectiveness and documentary use-value of his new model: 'How can the conceptual world of *Baal* possibly be made effectual in a world which nowhere conceptualizes the individual as a phenomenon, but as something to be taken for granted?'[7]

The scandal of *Baal* is the ubiquitous nature of the central figure's desire. The whole world is libidinized for Baal; he appears to have no sense of any boundaries, living in a flux of perceptual experience and continually seeking out situations of extreme limits which might bring new forms of subjective experience. This mode of being involves using others as objects for a catalyst for desire, rather than as ends in themselves: the libidinal aim is the desire of another, not the person as such, who becomes expendable once the circuit of desire is completed: 'When a woman, says Baal, gives you her all/Let her go, for she has nothing more.'[8] This libidinized world of pleasure and pain is seen retrospectively in the 'Chorale of the Great Baal', which precedes the play as a hymn to the real in which Baal lives and dies. Beauty and ugliness are indiscriminately experienced, and vice is as productive as virtue:

'All vices are good for something/And so is the man who practises them, says Baal.'[9] In the real everything is productive, nothing is wasted, and dirt (which, as Freud observed, is only matter in the wrong place) can become an object serving a non-squalid function. One of the lumber men in the forest who observed the onset of Baal's death comments: 'He had a way of laying himself down in the dirt; but then he never got up again and he knew it. He lay down as if in a bed already made.'[10]

For the desiring Baal there is nothing that is not there to be absorbed by his voracious senses. Indeed, the world is waiting for him before he arrives, mediated in the process of his growth in his mother's womb ('weissen Mutterschosse'), and retained by him as his body rots away in the womb of the earth ('dunklen Erden-schosse') (pp. 3 and 4). This cyclical process is theatricalized in Baal's 'chorale' (which addresses itself to the audience). The dominant image is the sky ('Himmel'), which is also the word for 'heaven' in German: metaphorically 'Himmel' stands for material nature, and it becomes a near-blasphemous paradox in its presence as mere cyclorama to desire. For Baal is inserted into a material process, where the presence of an indifferent nature is inescapable and indeed celebrated: he capitalizes on the indifference of nature by allowing himself total licence. The bare sky and the wide world form a steady backdrop, there before him and after him, giving the same cover in pleasure or pain. When Baal dies 'he has so much sky under his eyelids/That even in death he still has sky enough.'[11] Baal will have absorbed so much life that the difference between life and death becomes eroded.

Throughout the text, fragmentary scenes, clusters of images, and snatches of songs act as metaphors for a theatrical reality, access to which can only be got subjectively. The function of the subjective, however, is not that it acts as a precondition for a new reality, as the Expressionist project conceived it, but that it marks an attempt to get back to the concrete. By the same token, a Marxist reading which argues that all this is symptomatic of the fragmentariness of bourgeois life (see Knopf, 1980, p. 18), presupposes a unity which could be obtained if only things were otherwise. This is precisely what the material production of this text does not allow, for it shows a natural process where creatures prey on each other: the vultures wait for Baal and Baal knows it and preys on them in turn (p. 4). As the corpse of the woman who drowns herself because of him glides Ophelia-like downstream, far from leaving a gap in nature, her death facilitates other life:

101

Wrack and seaweed cling to her as she swims
Slowly their burden adds to her weight.
Coolly fishes play about her limbs
Creatures and growths encumber her in her final state.

[. . .]

As her pale body decayed in the water there
It happened (very slowly) that God gradually forgot it
First her face, then her hands, and right at the last her hair
Then she rotted in rivers where much else rotted.[12]

Snatches of elegies, celebrating the materiality of life and death, recur in the text, prominently as a contrast between the whiteness of bodies and fresh linen and the blackness of mud, earth, and filth, the delicacy of the woman and the grossness of Baal, all indiscriminately libidinized. The process of life is represented as an anti-narrative, a circulation of matter, where identities are always precarious and, if anything, shunned, because they interfere with participation in the process. Baal and his companions consciously seek to dissolve all boundaries, all naming: 'Yours is a face, in which the winds have room to blow . . . you haven't a face at all' (*GW* 1, pp. 42–3); 'When you've laid her ['*sie beschlafen hast*'], she may become a heap of flesh, which no longer has a face' (p. 11); 'D'you know what I'm called, then? My name's Sophie Barger.' 'You've got to forget it' (p. 26). *Baal* celebrates the circulation of desire irrespective of identities and personal destinies: 'As the juniper tree has many roots, all twisted, so you have many limbs in one bed, and in them the heart beats faster and the blood flows.'[13]

This imagery comes uncannily close to such postmodern conceptualizations as 'a body without organs', or 'rhizome' (Deleuze and Guattari, 1983), anti-categories which have been coined in order to open onto a project that seems very similar to that of the young Brecht, namely 'to overturn the theatre of representation into the order of desiring production' (Deleuze and Guattari, 1977, p. 271). To do this they reject psychoanalysis for what they call 'schizoanalysis', whose task it is to discover the nature of the libidinal investments in the social field. The 'rhizome' combats Aristotelian logic-trees that divide genera and species, and differentiae on a binary basis. Rhizomatic categories produce the heterogeneous, enabling the thinking of a-significant particles, not defined by a master signifier, but by the interaction

of flows and currents of desire. Schizoanalysis, as much the
author's as the reader's project, then serves as a new model for
artistic production, tracing 'lines of flight' which facilitate escape
out of the hierarchical system. The revolutionary reader/writer
(author and spectator each taking up this dual role) conducts
experiments, trying to find a way out of representation, providing
what Deleuze and Guattari call 'deterritorialized' images,
unformed material offering itself to temporary investments,
demolishing totalizing structures and revealing heterogeneous
elements. Desire flows and is constantly on the move, mapping
new territories, fluid boundaries that are constantly shifting.
Instead of a 'politics of interpretation' going over the past in the
realm of unconscious fantasy, they call for a 'politics of experimentation', taking hold of existing intensities of desire to get the
desiring mechanism in touch with historical reality (Guattari,
1984, pp. 82–107). By historical reality Deleuze and Guattari are
far from wanting to recover Œdipal experience; on the contrary,
what they are after is memory functioning as what they call a
'childhood block: it is the only real life of the child; it deter-
ritorializes; it displaces itself in time, with time, in order to reactivate desire and to multiply its connections' (Deleuze and
Guattari, 1976, p. 109).

There are traces in *Baal* which point towards the attempt to
recover such experience, manifesting themselves both in the energy
with which Baal sets about investing the world with new 'intensities',
'enjoyment, by God, is no easy thing' (*GW* 1, p. 4) ('Denn
Geniessen ist bei Gott nicht leicht!'), and in the few utopian elements
which involve the kind of past illuminations Deleuze and Guattari
have in mind. As at the age of twenty-five he begins to feel the onset
of his decline, he reminisces, declaring himself full of champagne
and happy in the dark, feeling 'nostalgia without memories':

Sick from the sun, and eaten raw by the weather
A looted wreath crowning his tangled head
He called back the dreams of a childhood he had lost altogether
Forgot the roof, but never the sky overhead.

[. . .]

Loafing through hells and flogged through paradises
Calm and grinning, with expressionless stare
Sometimes he dreams of a small field he recognizes
With blue sky overhead and nothing more.[14]

There is much that speaks *thematically* in the text against a simple appropriation of such traces as evidence of the utopian, not only Baal's exploitation of and brutality towards women and their readiness to lend themselves as victims, but also the collapse of his bravado and deliberate staging of his ignominious death. Yet formally, in the theatricalization of nature as the material rather than the ideal, the ambiguity of the social bond is exposed, a bond feared in life and desired in death, a reversal that subjects are exposed to in confronting concrete reality. Baal himself is quite unfitted as a character to give shape to the revolutionary impulse of this exposure even though he has access to the unrepresentable ground from which it springs, but in his undirected savagery he is the evidence of the unrepresentable, and there is a pathos in his failure to make use of it on behalf of the oppressed around him. Baal is unable to 'reactivate desire' and 'multiply connections'. He is the dialectic gone wild, his defeat a cautionary tale for revolutionaries. It is not surprising that Brecht had misgivings about his play 'lacking wisdom' and about its being useful as a blueprint.

In the Jungle of the Cities

It can be divulged here and now, that [this] drama, if it is to make progress at all, is bound to do so by stepping nonchalantly over the dead bodies of philologists.

Those in philological circles who are interested are hereby invited to ring back in eleven years or so.[15]

This play (referred to in future as *Jungle*), first performed in 1923, shares certain thematic features with *Baal*: a sordid milieu, a character or characters whose behaviour seems totally arbitrary, a sadistic attitude to female figures who are represented as wallowing in such treatment, a homosexual relation which culminates in death. It too is in the form of fragmented scenes, which were originally set in Chicago's Chinatown but extended to Chicago as a whole in the 1927 version (referred to here, as printed in the *Gesammelte Werke*). The action revolves around an apparently motiveless fight between an older and a younger man. The older man, the active agent in this play, is a Malayan timber merchant by the name of Shlink, who provokes a young American, George Garga, to enter into conflict with him, as a result of which Garga gets sacked from his job as a library assistant. In the course of their power struggle the economic fortunes of the contestants go back and forth, while Garga's family- and love-relations become pawns in the odd couple's all-absorbing master/slave game. Just as in *Baal*, the female figures readily offer themselves as victims to the power of the male. Shlink is eventually defeated in the struggle and dies by his own hand in the surrounding thickets and swamps. The conflict is played out against a sordid background, the scenes being set mainly in the workplaces and sleeping quarters of Shlink and Garga: lending library, timber merchant's office, Chinese hotel, the Gargas' home, a bar, and the wilderness surrounding Lake Michigan.

Brecht was as ambivalent with his utterances about this play as he was in the case of *Baal*. The only thing that is clear as one reads through the fragmentary notes he made over a period of time is that he was himself working towards an understanding of what he was trying to do. What was troubling him earlier and later is the nature of the fight that he is attempting to stage. He prefaced the play with an injunction to the audience not to worry their heads about the motives for the fight but to keep in mind what is at stake for the contestants, to make an impartial judgement on the technique of the fighters and to concentrate on the finish (*GW* 1, p. 126). But both at the time of the first performance and in his later retrospective notes on the early plays he feels he has to defend the lack of motive. He does not seem to be able to make up his mind whether it is a fight over material things, such as family and business, or whether it is a fight conducted for the sheer joy of fighting, but he does seem to be aware that the conflict is somehow overdetermined, that its source is not exhausted by a single factor:

> What was new was a type of man who conducted a fight without enmity but with hitherto unheard of (i.e. undepicted) methods, together with his attitude to the family, to marriage, to his fellow-humans in general, and much else – probably too much.[16]

Yet Brecht could not leave this 'too much' alone. In another set of notes to this play (*GW* 17, pp. 969–72) he wavers most interestingly between maintaining that there is such a thing as fighting for pure enjoyment — he calls it an 'idealized fight' (p. 970) ('einen idealen Kampf'), in contrast to the fight over women or property so common in the bourgeois theatre – and wondering whether this 'idealized fight' with which he was so fascinated might not be an allegory of the class struggle, which

105

would make it into a revolutionary fight instead of a competition for what was going in capitalism.

What Brecht returns to again and again in his comments is the idea of a furious fight engaged in for no other reason than the pure pleasure of fighting, a kind of 'mythic fight' conducted only for the sake of determining who was the 'best man' (*GW* 17, pp. 98–9). Yet there is no indication that the contestants experience their fight as an enjoyable sport; on the contrary, they show every sign of being caught up in a paranoiac structure. If this is a sport it is only so to the extent that it is a struggle about who can torment the other most. It is not so much about the pleasure of winning as about the seemingly perverse pleasure of destroying or being destroyed. It ends with Shlink dying ignominiously (like Baal), with Garga proclaiming that the most important thing is not to win, but to stay alive (p. 188).

So what gives this fight its energy, if it is not, as Brecht would like it to have been, the sheer love of fighting? Someone (Garga) is unreasonably provoked and yet quick to take up the challenge, taking up the fight 'unconditionally' (p. 138) ('*unverbindlich*'). This includes his acceptance of Shlink's terms, that he is to play the evil master in a master/slave relationship, which Shlink defines:

> From now on, Mr Garga, my fate's in your hands. I don't know you! From now on I'm going to be your slave. Every look that comes into your eyes will trouble me. Every one of your wishes, known or unknown, will find me willing. Your cares will be my cares, my strength will be yours. My feelings will be dedicated to you alone, and you will be an evil master.[17]

The staging of conflicts and quarrels works as part of a theatrical moment in the constitution and reconstitution of subjectivity and again bears out Lacan's theory of the formation of the subject. That which gives rise to that particular form of aggression he terms 'aggressivity' is the fear of disintegration, the threat to the body image posed by the supposed unity and wholeness of another: 'Subjective experience must be fully enabled to recognize the central nucleus of ambivalent aggressivity, which in the present stage of our culture is given to us under the dominant species of *resentment*' (Lacan, 1977a, p. 20). It is not my intention to apply Lacan's theory to Brecht's text in an instrumental fashion, but merely to point to certain paranoiac structures and images of disintegration which might make an otherwise motiveless fight between 'comrades of a metaphysical action' (*GW* 1, p. 186) more readable in terms of the text's own figurations:

SHLINK . . . You wanted me dead. But I wanted a fight. Not of the flesh but of the spirit.

GARGA And the mind, you see, is nothing. The important thing is not to be stronger, but to come off alive. I can't defeat you, I can only stamp you into the ground.[18]

In *Jungle* the dominant images are clustered around the fear of losing face, and these images are shared out among the characters and are not confined to the main protagonists. Unlike in *Baal* dissolution is feared rather than desired, but as in *Baal* the male figures constitute themselves at the expense of the female ones who again masochistically turn themselves into sex objects. The obsessive dwelling on the face as a likely index to identity is contrapuntally present throughout and provides one of the few conceptual links in the otherwise non-narrative stance of the play. It is partly by this means that the fear of disintegration is made representable.

Dramatically the text is made up of a series of face-losing encounters within a paranoiac structure of pursuers and victims. The opening scene immediately strikes this double note in that the challenger, Shlink, seems to have a sufficient knowledge of Garga's life to mock, harass, and hustle him. Shlink is well informed as regards the whereabouts and abject circumstances of Garga's father John, his mother Mae, his sister Marie, and girl-friend Jane, and even about Garga's private dream, his longing to go to Tahiti, factors which empower his persecution:

GARGA Are you running a detective agency? Your interest in us is flattering, I hope.

SHLINK You're just shutting your eyes. Your family is headed for disaster. You're the only one who makes any money, and you can indulge in opinions! When you could be on your way to Tahiti. *Shows him a sea chart that he has with him.*[19]

He taunts him with ever-increasing sums of money in a deliberate move to provoke and humiliate him:

GARGA What do you want of me? I don't know you. I've never seen you before.

SHLINK I never heard of this book and it doesn't mean a thing to me. I'm offering you forty dollars for your opinion of it.

GARGA I'll sell you the opinions of Mr J. V. Jensen and Mr
          Arthur Rimbaud, but I won't sell you my opinion.
SHLINK Your opinion is as worthless as theirs, but right now
          I want to buy it.
GARGA I indulge in opinions.[20]

As a result of Shlink's manoeuvres Garga is dismissed. In order
to save his face and his family he now has no option but to take
over the timber business which Shlink forces on him. The persecution and its effects on the driven set of characters manifests itself
not merely on a thematic and fragmentary narrative level, but via
a persistent set of configurations which orchestrate the sufferings
undergone by all as they literally face humiliation, rejection,
hunger, sickness, and death. As already mentioned, the most
prominent metaphor is that of losing face, which recurs in a
variety of sensuous images whose meaning and connection are
withheld: 'May I see your face?'/'It's no longer a face. It isn't me'
(p. 181); 'People stay what they are even when their faces
disintegrate' (p. 182); 'My mother, Mae Garga . . . went missing
three years ago in October and has even vanished from memory,
she no longer has a face. It fell off like a yellow leaf' (p. 185).

The list can be extended. Causing another to lose face seems to
act as some guarantee of identity. A Salvation Army officer who
stands to make a gain for his cause maintains, 'I have always kept
my face clean', only to have Garga incite Shlink to 'spit in his face
. . . if it so pleases you', as the price for receiving the gift (p.
143). Shlink relates how he was maltreated working in the junks
on the Yangtze, 'a man trod on our faces every time he came on
board. We were too lazy to move our faces out of the way. Somehow or other the man was never too lazy' (p. 154). One of the
women's faces is described as looking like 'a lemon ice that's starting to thaw' (p. 163), another asks 'does my face seem bloated
to you?' (p. 191). Shlink describes Garga's face as 'hard as amber,
transparent, here and there one can find dead flies in it' (p. 186).
Shlink begs Marie, 'throw a cloth over my face, have pity', just
before he dies (p. 192).

When they finally confront each other in the undergrowth and
gravel pits of the lakeside it is only Shlink who is still committed
to the metaphysics of the conflict, and who mourns the impossibility of a bodily relation, whether it is grounded in love or hate,
and the divisions in language which make personal communication
impossible (p. 187). Garga divests himself of all responsibilities

and sets off alone to begin again in a new city. Like Baal he
affirms the past, regretting nothing: 'It's a good thing to be alone.
The chaos is spent. That was the best time' (p. 62).[21] Chaos is
good, because it leads back to the concrete, out of the repressive
representation, but only for the male protagonist, to which the text
testifies: 'You have opened her eyes to the fact that she will always
be an object for men' (p. 164). Women are no more than props
in the maintenance of the men's solipsistic fight; they have to
submit to the constant masculine desire for representation together
with the fear of feminine excess. But whereas in *Baal* the themes
and figures of the text incline towards a celebration of dissolution
and a defiance in the face of decay, in *Jungle* dissolution, decay,
and death are feared and fought by all. Both plays, however, are
preoccupied with the concrete, figured as uncontrollable bodily
fluids – spittle, tears – or bodily grossness and sickness in the
ravages of time: what is shown is the uncanniness of disintegration
rather than the comforts of metamorphosis. Being is in the body;
the subject is preoccupied with evolving a bodily image of itself.
The body therefore becomes highly libidinized, the effect of which
is aggressivity as a reaction to the threat of bodily disintegration,
loss of continuity, or loss of self-esteem. The characters under
subjection to this threat are put to the utmost test in their attempts
to form a libidinal relationship to the world (Baal) or test out its
constancy (Shlink). Narcissism and identification emerge as part of
the conflict with an other, as each tries to verify itself by trying
to take the other's place (Shlink and Garga). Narcissism (fear of
losing face) is not a mere pathology (Brecht's worry in case *Jungle*
was psychologized) but part of self-formation, in that it provides
a conceptual link between fragmentation and unity, bodily relations and language. The source of energy, the 'metaphysical'
element in both plays, is narcissistic passion, the goal of energy
being the interaction with an other (mirror image) rather than
with the Other (the power structure). Yet the Other is clearly
present in the theatricalization of the general oppressiveness of the
living and working conditions of the characters and in the
language which cannot articulate their concrete experience.

These plays pose a challenge to the spectator, and even more
to the reader, who misses out on the stage production on which
these texts depend perhaps more than any other of Brecht's plays.
The spectator needs to be drawn into the production process in
order to experience the shifting and contradictory choices of stage
subjects/objects. The work of engaging the audience is not done on

the stage via specific V-effects, but pressure is put on the audience to co-produce in order to avoid the unpalatable alternative of placing her- or himself in a psychotic position and abandoning meaning.

Notes

Since completing the manuscript for this book, I have read Linda Hutcheon's *A Poetics of Postmodernism: History, Theory, Fiction* and found the first reference to Brecht as someone who should be assessed in a postmodern context, since his work makes crucial such issues as the political dimensions of self-reflexivity, the problematization of self and history, and the calculated decentring of text and audience (1988, pp. 218–22). In particular she stresses that 'postmodernism has indeed used a version of the Brechtian model' in that postmodern texts 'decode themselves by foregrounding their own contradictions' (pp. 210, 211).

1 'Der den grossen Sprung machen will, muss einige Schritte zurückgehen. Das Heute geht gespeist durch das Gestern in das Morgen' (*GW* 17, p. 952).
2 'Im Kampf mit den alten (Problemen) gewinnen die neuen Ideen ihre schärfsten Formulierungen' (*GW* 17, p. 952).
3 'Das Stück *Baal* mag denen, die nicht gelernt haben, dialektisch zu denken, allerhand Schwierigkeiten bereiten. Sie werden darin kaum etwas anderes als die Verherrlichung nackter Ichsucht erblicken' (*GW* 17, p. 947).
4 There are five versions of *Baal*, stretching from 1918 to 1955, plus a fragment (see Schmidt, 1969).
5 Seen by some critics as a Verlaine/Rimbaud figure (see review in Schmidt, 1969, pp. 173–4).
6 'Ich schreibe an einer Komödie: "Baal frisst! Baal tanzt!! Baal verklärt sich!!!" Da kommt ein Hamster drin vor, ein ungeheurer Genüssling, ein Kloss, der am Himmel Fettflecken hinterlässt, ein maitoller Bursche mit unsterblichen Gedärmen' (Schmidt, 1969, p. 95).
7 'Wie soll die Vorstellungswelt etwa des Stückes "Baal" zur Wirkung gebracht werden können, in einer Welt, in deren Vorstellungen das Individuum keineswegs ein Phänomen, sondern das Selbstverständliche ist' (Schmidt, 1969, p. 105).
8 'Gibt ein Weib, sagt Baal, euch alles her/Lasst es fahren, denn sie hat nicht mehr' (*GW* 1, p. 4). All references are to the last version of the play, published 1955.
9 'Alle Laster sind zu etwas gut/Und der Mann auch, sagt Baal, der sie tut' (*GW* 1, p. 4).
10 'Er hatte eine Art, sich hinzulegen in den Dreck; dann stand er ja nimmer auf, und dass wusste er. Er legte sich wie in ein gemachtes Bett' (*GW* 1, p. 67).

11 'Soviel Himmel hat Baal unterm Lid/Dass er tot noch grad gnug
Himmel hat' (*GW* 1, p. 4).

12

Tang und Algen hielten sich an ihr ein
So dass sie langsam viel schwerer ward
Kühl die Fische schwammen an ihrem Bein:
Pflanzen und Tiere beschwerten noch ihre letzte Fahrt.

[. . .]

Als ihr bleicher Leib im Wasser verfaulet war
Geschah es, sehr langsam, dass Gott sie allmählich vergass:
Erst ihr Gesicht, dann die Hände und ganz zuletzt erst ihr Haar.
Dann ward sie Aas in Flüssen mit vielem Aas.

(*GW* 1, p. 53; *CP* 1, pp. 47 and 48)

13 'Wie der Machandelbaum viele Wurzeln hat, verschlungene, so habt
ihr viele Glieder in einem Bett, und darinnen schlagen Herzen und
Blut fliesst durch' (*GW* 1, p. 11).

14

Von Sonne krank und ganz von Regen zerfressen
Geraubter Lorbeer im zerrauften Haar
Hat er seine ganze Jugend, nur nicht ihre Träume vergessen
Lange das Dach! nie den Himmel, der drüber war.

[. . .]

Schlendernd durch Höllen und gepeitscht durch Paradiese
Still und grinsend, vergehenden Gesichts
Träumt er gelegentlich von einer kleinen Wiese
Mit blauem Himmel drüber und sonst nichts.

(*GW* 1, pp. 60 and 61; *CP* 1, pp. 54 and 55)

15

Jetzt schon kann ihnen freilich verraten werden, dass das Drama,
wenn es überhaupt schreiten sollte, in jedem Fall mit Gelassenheit
über die Leichen der Philologen schreiten wird.

Interessenten aus Philologenkreisen müssen also ersucht werden
in etwa elf Jahren wieder anzurufen. (*GW* 17, p. 969)

16

Neu war ein Typus Mensch, der einen Kampf ohne Feindschaft
mit bisher unerhörten, dass heisst noch nicht gestalteten Methoden
führte, und seine Stellung gegen die Familie, zur Ehe, überhaupt
zum Mitmenschen und vieles mehr; im Grund natürlich zu viel.
(*GW* 15, p. 67; *CP* 1, p. 434)

17

Von heute ab, Mr Garga, lege ich mein Geschick in Ihre Hände.
Sie sind mir unbekannt. Von heute ab bin ich ihre Kreatur. Jeder
Blick ihrer Augen wird mich beunruhigen. Jeder Ihrer Wünsche,

auch der unbekannte, wird mich willfährig finden. Ihre Sorge ist meine Sorge, meine Kraft wird die Ihre sein. Meine Gefühle werden nur Ihnen gewidmet, und sie werden böse sein. (*GW* 1, p. 138; *CP* 1, p. 129)

18 SHLINK . . . Sie wollten mein Ende, aber ich wollte den Kampf. Nicht das Körperliche, sondern das Geistige war es.

  GARGA Und das Geistige, das sehen Sie, das ist nichts. Es ist nicht wichtig, der Stärkere zu sein, sondern der Lebendige. Ich kann Sie nicht besiegen, ich kann Sie nur in den Boden stampfen. (*GW* 1, p. 190; *CP* 1, p. 175)

19 GARGA Haben Sie ein Detektivbüro? Ihr Interesse für uns ist hoffentlich schmeichelhaft.

  SHLINK Sie kneifen einfach die Augen zu. Die Familienkatastrophe ist unaufhaltsam. Nur Sie verdienen und Sie leisten sich Ansichten. Dabei könnten Sie nach Tahiti fahren. (*Zeigt ihm eine mitgebrachte Seekarte*). (*GW* 1, p. 130; *CP* 1, p. 122)

20 GARGA Was wollen Sie von mir? Ich kenne Sie nicht, habe Sie nie gesehen.

  SHLINK Ich biete Ihnen vierzig Dollar für Ihre Ansicht über dieses Buch, das ich nicht kenne und das gleichgültig ist.

  GARGA Ich verkaufe Ihnen Ansichten von M. V. Jensen und Mr Arthur Rimbaud, aber ich verkaufe Ihnen nicht meine Ansicht darüber.

  SHLINK Und auch Ihre Ansicht ist gleichgültig, ausser, dass ich sie kaufen will.

  GARGA Ich leiste mir aber Ansichten. (*GW* 1, p. 128; *CP* 1, pp. 119–20)

21 'Allein sein ist eine gute Sache. Das Chaos ist aufgebraucht. Es war die beste Zeit' (*GW* 1, p. 193; *CP* 1, p. 178).

6

The Brechtian postmodern

To explain Brecht's significance for and in the postmodern theatre he needs to be seen in conjunction with the work of other writers and theorists of the theatre. It is a fact that the continuing effects of Brecht's radical theory of the epic theatre cannot be found in the practical realization of his own plays, at least not in the reverent way that producers are made to treat them at present. Hence we have arrived at the paradoxical situation of a 'Brecht-reception without Brecht' (see Wirth, 1980, p. 16). That is to say, his most radical ideas, as he tried to develop them in his early and more marginal works, have not been allowed to fertilize his main oeuvre.

Brecht himself had always regarded the epic theatre as a transitional phenomenon, as a necessary compromise within the framework of the bourgeois institution; this is why he distinguished between a contemporary theatre in the epic mode as an example of a 'minor pedagogy' and a learning theatre of the future as an example of a 'major pedagogy' (see Chapter 1). He had hoped for his epic theatre to be revolutionary enough to prepare the ground for a radically subversive dramaturgy, but it is all too clear that the combination of social criticism and epic form which he advocated so forcefully did not work in the way he envisaged. What happened instead, as more than one critic has pointed out, is that the epic idiom, itself at the centre of avant-garde movements from the early part of the century onwards (Servos, 1981, p. 438), has become the universal language of contemporary theatre, irrespective of its ideological origin (Wirth, 1980). The techniques of montage, of epic narration, of diverse visual and auditory effects, are used far more radically than they are in Brecht's own plays. Today Brecht's enormous effect has to be seen on the level of a continuing formal invention, in the way his theoretical precepts appear in praxis, particularly as regards the question of stage dialogue, traditionally the *raison d'être* of drama. In his reconstruction of the history of the drama, Peter Szondi uses the term 'absolute drama' to define the drama of modernity as one whose sole constitutive element was the reproduction of interpersonal relations on the stage, with both dramatist and spectator totally excluded: 'The lines in a play are as little an address to the spectator as they are a declaration by the author.' The dramatist 'does not speak; he institutes discussion . . . the theatregoer is an observer – silent, with hands tied, lamed by the impact of this other world' (Szondi, 1987, p. 8).

Brecht was aware of the uses of dialogue in propping up a preconceived reality. By means of a variety of disjunctive techniques and devices he did his best to abandon dialogue in favour of discourse, even where he most wanted to achieve a didactic effect. He moved from a stale communication between character and character to a technique of turning to the interested party: in his paradigm of epic theatre, *The Street Scene* (see Chapter 2) the demonstrator turns to his fellow-performers on the street. Wherever Brecht used dialogue he used it in a critical subversive way, showing that the speaker's voice did not originate in a pure and pristine selfhood, but was the effect of an intersection of many codes. The *Lehrstücke*, the early plays, the fragment *Fatzer*, are all evidence that Brecht's theatre provided the impulse for the dissolution of traditional stage dialogue. Moreover, his theory points forcefully to the fact that theatrical utterance is made up of a contradictory structure of verbal, gestural, and auditory elements and is far from being merely a literary mode of speech. His epic theory thus led to a dramatic form based on a semiotic understanding of theatrical practice, a non-narrative, non-representational theatre, in which the traditional forms, genres, and practices of the theatre fall apart and the professional distinctions of actor, playwright, director, stage manager, scene shifter, spectator are eroded: 'Postmodern theatre and *mise en scène* abandon their textual and dramaturgical inheritance, the better to absorb the performance tradition – in particular, the unique and ephemeral event of the theatricalization of the stage utterance' (Pavis, 1986). The fictitious unity between voice and word is shown up by making speech compete with other elements on the stage, such as music, sound effects, gestures, sets, props, lighting, mime, mask, costume (Finter, 1983).

Performance in this sense is not confined to the playing of a part on the stage: 'Conceived as an art-form at the juncture of other signifying practices as varied as dance, music, painting, architecture, and sculpture, performance seems paradoxically to correspond on all counts to the new theatre invoked by Artaud' (Féral, 1982, pp. 170–1). The most significant features of performance are the subjection of the body to analysis, the use of space as an experimental object, and the disturbance of certain boundaries, namely those between artist and spectator, spectator and art 'object', art 'object' and artist.

Performance is the radical refunctioning of the theatre which Brecht could not undertake, committed as he was to the spectator's discovery of his own contradictory production process via a theatre of consciousness. Nevertheless in the examples of the new theatricality and its use of the techniques of performance that follow a subversive form of epic theatre will become apparent. In the theatrical experiments of Beckett, Gombrowicz, and Grotowski in Europe, and Chaikin, Foreman, and Wilson in the USA, the combined influence of Brecht and Artaud makes itself felt in the way that the form of involving or implicating the audience has become the basic structure of contemporary drama, although this may rarely take the strategic form of a direct address.

Expropriating Brecht: the dance theatre of Pina Bausch

The work of Pina Bausch has been well known in Europe and America since 1973, when she took over the direction of the dance theatre in Wuppertal, a small town in the Ruhr.[1] Bausch has only recently been given some prominence in Britain through a series of three Channel 4 television programmes: *1980 – A Piece by Pina Bausch*, shown 1984; *Bluebeard – While Listening to a Tape Recording of Béla Bartok's Opera 'Duke Bluebeard's Castle'*, shown 1985; *Café Müller*, shown 1987. The first programme (recorded on the company's first, and to my knowledge, only visit to England, in 1982) was supplemented with an illuminating introduction by Susan Sontag, entitled 'A Prima for Pina', on which I will draw for some preliminary remarks, before going on to a more theoretical exposition. Bausch's work is uniquely suited to serve as a kind of transition point between the predominantly narrative theatre of Brecht and those experimental theatres which have abandoned all forms of narration.

Pina Bausch was trained as a dancer in Germany and the United States, and worked in both places for many years, first as a dancer and then as a choreographer, until she made her most important début at the age of thirty-three as dancer, director, and choreographer of her own dance theatre, composed of about twenty-six dancers representing many different nationalities. One of the sequences performed by them consists of dancers coming to the front of the stage and shouting out three national items by which their country can be identified, to the recorded tune of 'Land of Hope and Glory': 'Queen! Police! Tea!', 'Geisha! Honda! Harakiri!', 'Spaghetti! Caruso! Espresso!'. There are no stars in Bausch's company, nor any specific parts to be performed: the dancer-cum-actors are asked to play themselves by means of improvisation, producing material around a given emotion. Where Brecht got his actors to work with and 'show' invented emotions, Bausch and her company work with real, often extreme emotion, coming from real, not illusory bodies. The body-language initially derives from unconscious sources, but once a particular sequence has been sufficiently explored and shaped in rehearsal it is then performed in its set form.

Bausch not only works with real emotion; she also works with real time. One of the characteristics of her performances are the many repetitions of rituals and actions performed at various and varying speeds. As Susan Sontag points out, taking one example, by the time one of her dancers has run round the room fifty times calling out 'I'm tired', that person is *really* tired. This use of subjective time rather than historical time dissolves the normal space–time boundaries: time becomes de-reified with the result that the spectator will feel this experience in his/her own body.

The subject-matter of Bausch's work is loss or anxiety, often revealed by the dancers' enactment of childlike fears in childish games and ritual, sometimes all playing at children, sometimes playing adults and children.[2] In the piece called *1980* there is a particularly powerful scenario which runs like a musical theme through the performance. A man sitting limp and passive has a woman fitting silk stockings onto his legs, applying make-up, and generally handling him as a fetishized object; in a second sequence a woman is kissing a man all over his face, disfiguring him with the imprints of her lipstick; in a third sequence a woman, again the active figure, is cradling a man curled up like an infant on her lap, fondling him and looking up at intervals with a sly conspiratorial gaze. The woman's look is presented as a conscious deceit when it is really unconscious. She does not know she is seducing the 'child' any more than the woman in the second example knows she is bruising the man. These are not mimetic acts, but conscious looks stand for unconscious desire. The scenarios are orchestrated by a lack of fit between stage décor, recorded music, actors' speech, and actors' body-language: the woman's seductive handling of the 'child' goes on to the tender tune of Brahms's lullaby, in which mother, God, and angels are all promising the infant full protection.

Pina Bausch has rejected the idea that her work is in any sense specifically feminist, although a strong theme of her work is the oppression and commodification of women in a society ruled by men. Often, however, she tends to show that women themselves collude in the oppression of women: a woman pins another woman against the wall, taping her in place by strands of her hair and corners of her clothing, so that she has to remain there spread-eagled for the rest of a long scene. On the whole, however, she reveals the masquerades that both sexes have to perform in order to survive as gendered subjects. There are brilliant hysterical performances by men and women: a man pirouettes around dressed as a ballerina, shouting hoarsely: 'I'll show you! I'll show you!', doing entrechats which reveal pink underskirts and blue panties; in another piece (Bausch's works tend to cross-refer and even quote from each other) a powerfully built woman dressed in a bathing suit struts up and down the stage yelling defiantly at the audience, doing an inventory of the parts of her body, trying to resist the cultural code. This latter act ends with her sitting at a table avidly taking bites out of a large apple, monotonously reciting 'one for Jan, one for Mechthild' (members of the company, hence her family), while spitting out large gobbets of the fruit all over the place. So, as often in Bausch's theatre, we are back in the childhood scenario again, that final and precarious refuge where the players discover the banal failures behind which they and we hide our anxieties and aggressions.

Bausch's works are long, often up to three or four hours, but they do not make up a totality in the German sense of a *Gesamtkunstwerk* ('total work of art'), the way that Wagner conceived his operas. Bausch works with a variety of theatrical genres – dance, which might include some classical balletic movements in both a parodic and non-parodic way, recorded music and song, mime – but the autonomy of the individual media is preserved and the resulting dissonances are exploited. She uses the principle of montage – the associative but discontinuous linkage of scenic material – as the structural principle for both the form and content of her work. The way she uses the epic idiom is thus different from the bulk of Brecht's work (always excepting the early plays and the *Lehrstücke*), in which the disruptions of the form were generally held together by the content of the *Fabel*. In Bausch's theatre there is no unity and no centring of the action: it is impossible to see all that is going on at once because so much is going on simultaneously, a classic procedure in the postmodern performing arts. The spectator never feels sure that s/he is looking at the 'right' place, since the principal action always seems to go on off-centre. The 'normal' voyeuristic modes of sorting out the world are thus exposed and deconstructed: the onlooker begins to feel the force of his/her own determining fantasies.

The startling effect of Bausch's dance theatre resides in the constant lack of fit between the stage décor, the recorded music, the actor's speech, and the actor's body-language. The stage may be covered with a variety of natural materials, whose sound and smell can be perceived – leaves, flowers, damp earth, grass, water – which set the tone and mood of a particular piece. The music used varies from classical to popular, the latter mainly pieces and songs from the late 1920s and 1930s. A set piece of the company's performance shows them engaged in a collective act of moving round and round the stage and through the auditorium in their standard costume, the women dressed in the glossy, soft, and clinging materials of the time and wearing high heels, executing to an obsessively catchy tune a series of most oddly contradictory and repetitive body movements, consisting of stiffly circling elbows and exaggeratedly gyrating hips, the men following with their own awkwardly restrained movements, dressed in formal suits and shiny shoes. This forms a kind of grand collective counter-piece to the eternal coupling and uncoupling movements the sexes engage in during the rest of the performance, in which the woman darts forward to cling and embrace, the man violently rejects and repulses, or each violently assaults the other, dozens of times at increasing speed, until each clings helplessly to the other in a brief moment of real exhaustion. Meanwhile the music drones on with some sentimental refrain, parodically accompanying the out-rageous actions.

Pina Bausch's dance theatre has been designated the 'Theatre of Experience' (Servos, 1981) to mark it off as an emancipatory form of dance, opposed to the strict control of classical ballet, with its emotion only recollected in tranquillity. As theatre it also contrasts with Brecht, because her use of body signs implicates the subjectivity of her actors as real people, whose experience counts, irrespective of their ideological commitment (her multi-national company would seem to be a testimony to this). It is in this sense that one can see her work, which uses some of the basic concepts of epic theatre – *gestus*, V-effect, a certain employment of the comic as a sudden switch of gestalt – as an expropriation of the work of Brecht, because her political goals (which she would not describe as such) are different, even though she occupies the same philosophical ground as he does in her desire to *show* people as they really are. The difference is that her actors show themselves; the split they enact between body and social role is experienced and enacted on their own bodies. They are the demonstrators of their own bodies, not the body of some passer-by, as in Brecht's street-scene model. What difference does this make?

An obvious example from which to generalize the difference is Bausch's rendering of Brecht's *The Seven Deadly Sins of the Petit-Bourgeois* (discussed in Chapter 5), performed at Wuppertal in 1976. Bausch's Anna 2 cannot merely stand as a parable for the average man/woman who toils to produce the goods for the consumption of the capitalist Other and who turns her/himself into a commodity in the process; it is rather the violence perpetrated on the individual female body by men, and by other women, that is here starkly foregrounded:

> Images, which stick in one's mind: how Anna 1 combs out Anna 2's hair, as if grooming a horse, cutting off a great swath at the end, as if castrating her . . . how she then pulls off her clothes and at once stuffs her into new ones, puts red pumps on her and paints her lips – her first painful experience with a press photographer – men who want to see something for their money, who grope and fumble at her and shove her from one to the other . . . the pathetic row of girls, each scraggier than the next . . . again and again the courage to have long pauses without any music. (Wyss, 1977, p. 164)

Moreover, as the review stresses, the two Annas are physically as different as can be, each built to be out of key with her role – Anna 2, the dancer, is plump and ungainly, Anna 1, the singer and instigator, is slight, with a croaking voice, as much victim as her 'sister', each more sinned against than sinning. The effect of these scenarios is thus to render palpable the general tension between personal desire and the demands society (the family who exact the money) makes on the woman to give up her own creative being and offer herself up as a sacrifice. In Brecht's version, of course, the attack is on a form of repression that arises out of a particular historical situation: what is categorized as 'sin', sloth, pride, anger, etc., is merely a threat to the capitalist economy. In Bausch's version the 'sin' of prostitution appears as all the deadlier for leading to a compulsive surrender of subjectivity in order to placate the Other, who is shown (via the *gestus* of the performers) not only to be dwelling within the subject as represented by the actor, as in Brecht, but in the actual bodies of the people on stage.

Clearly Bausch's aim is not that of transmitting knowledge rationally, by presenting the spectator with a *Fabel*, in the style of Brecht. Her V-effects contain no guide to interpretation via various programmatic texts, nor do her actors comport themselves with a conscious understanding of their role *vis-à-vis* one another. In the article, 'Performance and theatricality: the subject demystified', Féral (1982) shows that the essential material of the new theatricality is bodily movement in space, and hence the body in all its aspects will become the focus of performance, a source of continual upsetting and ironizing of gesture, voice, role, action, custom, and timing. In addition there will be a rending of secure backgrounds, not only resulting in kinesic effects from the challenging of our assumptions of bodily positions in space (idealized in classical dance) but also from the disruption of settings, the cosy contexts upon which much human meaning and power is based. Stable selves disappear; intelligible contexts metamorphose unaccountably, foregrounding the vulnerability of the subject and its feeble defences. Repetitions, the basis of all roles, all laws (as Brecht wants to demonstrate in his street-scene model), will be shown to be different at every occurrence. Difference will negate sameness both from one time to the next and from one space to the next. Symbolic structures depend on repetitions, but the difference of each subject invades the boundaries of these repetitions:

> Theatricality can therefore be seen as composed of two different parts: one highlights performance and is made up of the *realities of the imaginary*; and the other highlights the theatrical and is made up of *specific symbolic structures*. The former originates within the subject and allows his flows of desire to speak; the latter inscribes the subject in the law and in theatrical codes, which is to say, in the symbolic. Theatricality arises from the play between these two realities. From then on it is necessarily a theatricality tied to a desiring subject, a fact which no doubt accounts for our difficulty in defining it. Theatricality cannot *be*, it must be *for* someone. In other words, it is *for the Other*. (Féral, 1982, p. 178)

But whereas Brecht is mainly concerned with the symbolic effects impinging on the subject who is inserted in a historically specific structure, Bausch is interested in the way the subject suffers from the confinement of its imaginary by *any* symbolic structure and the results this produces. She shows the distortions of the imaginary as an effect of social oppression but without specifically identifying the causes; she is engaged in writing the discontinuous history of that oppression and in uncovering the traces of the violence of repression which continually keeps it in place. What Féral writes of the objectives of the performing element of theatricality, citing other examples, also goes for the dynamics of Bausch's work:

> Such demonstrations, which are brought to the surface more or less violently by the performer, are presented to the Other's view, to the view of others, in order that they may undergo a collective verification. Once this exploration of the body, and therefore of the subject, has been completed, and once certain repressions have been brought to light, objectified, and represented, they are frozen under the gaze of the spectator, who appropriates them as a form of knowledge. (Féral, 1982, p. 172)

In its concentration on an authorless, actorless, directorless theatre, in no way subordinated to a literary text, Pina Bausch's dance theatre is an expropriation of Brecht's epic-cum-dialectical theatre: 'Dance mobilizes the modes of presenting emotions as its own unique contribution to the predominantly rational-cognitive communication of Brechtian theatre' (Servos, 1981, p. 445). Where Brecht analysed the great historical process, 'the Dance Theatre shows how the influence of these processes reaches down into the concrete individual realm', making visible 'the body conventions internalized *via* anxieties' (*ibid.*). This is also what I see as going on in Brecht's early plays, but in neither case does this process include a clear political dimension, except in as far as the body is always also a body politic, a body inscribed in a social system. The collective awakening of the audience to its own repression is certainly a more radical move than Freud's cautious sublimatory strategies when it comes to art. How political the discourse of the body can be (while avoiding a metaphysics of the body in the style of Artaud) will be the subject of discussion via the work of Heiner Müller.

Refunctioning Brecht: the shocks of Heiner Müller

Heiner Müller (born in 1929) may be seen as representative of the way the postmodern theatre has absorbed the performance tradition in order to do something different from the dramatists of high modernism in whose wake but not whose shadow he is working. In a homage to the work of Pina Bausch, Müller writes – in the form of a long lyric fragment – that the mythical space she has created in her dance theatre is one where history is merely a disturbance, 'like flies in summer', buzzing in the background. This space, threatened by the occupation of either of two existing 'grammars', that of ballet or drama, is defended by the 'line of flight' of the dance, which serves as a protection against both invasions (Müller, 1981, p. 35). It is thus the performance aspect of Bausch's work which Müller admires, having himself absorbed the performance tradition over the years in order to break out of the established codes and away from the work of high modernism.

Müller is the dramatist who is now generally regarded, both by his own often ambivalent admission and by the assessment of others, as the most obvious successor to Brecht.[3] 'Successor' here is emphatically not meant in the sense of preserver of a heritage, for Müller has a profane view of what it entails to be in a position of 'belatedness', to speak with Harold Bloom, appearing not to suffer from the anxiety of influence. On the contrary, he has declared loud and clear that 'to use Brecht without criticizing him is a betrayal'.[4]

Many lines of this book come together in Müller's work. The aim of this section is to use Müller as a pivot for the issues of what a postmodern political art might look like or does look like, rather than contribute to an assessment of his work as such.[5] I shall begin by giving a brief account of his position as a political writer in the GDR, move on to discuss his position as a writer for the theatre in Brecht's wake, taking *Mauser* as an example of his revision of the *Lehrstück*, and finally turn to his more recent practice, via a brief account of the theatre of Robert Wilson, who co-staged *Hamletmaschine*. I hope then to be in a position to make some summarizing remarks on the politics of the post-avant-garde theatre.

Problems of commitment

Müller's life and art easily exhibit as many contradictions as those of Brecht (see Chapter 1, p. 9). He lives in East Berlin, yet now

122

has free access to West Berlin and the West in general, where his work is most frequently performed and from where he presumably derives most of his income. He firmly believes that the revolutionary author's task is to work towards his own dissolution, yet he is privileged in having an unprecedented degree of freedom precisely because he is Heiner Müller. This is one of the abiding contradictions we are left with while the 'death of the author' (Barthes, Foucault) continues to be a non-event that is grossly exaggerated. His privileged status is nevertheless a fact and ironically in keeping with 'The Father's Image as Destiny' (see Müller and Heinitz, 1984). History also repeats itself in that the critical reception in both East and West tends to polarize Müller's achievement. The East has come to recognize the provocative nature of his work, but is hesitant to subscribe to his radical aesthetics, fearing these might end up serving the capitalist cause: the West tends to treat him either as a doctrinaire Marxist, spinning political allegories to justify the GDR, or as a highly gifted creative writer, whose political commitment is secondary.[6]

Müller has written some thirty plays in about thirty years. In the 1950s and early 1960s he encountered difficulties with his work, because he chose to focus on Germany's subjective involvement with fascism at a time when the GDR wanted to regard the anti-fascist democratic revolt as completed so that it could concentrate its forces on the construction of a socialist state.[7] In *The Slaughter* (*Die Schlacht*, 1951–74), written around Brecht's play *Fear and Misery of the Third Reich* (1935–8), Müller shows how the average citizen was implicated in the horrors of fascism. When later on in the 1950s he began to question the conditions necessary for a socialist transformation of history in a more concrete way, his staging of conflictual situations, as, for example in *Tractor* (*Traktor*, 1955–61), and his use of theatre as a laboratory for social fantasies offended against the harmonizing tendencies of the prevailing code of socialist realism. In the late 1960s and early 1970s he produced a series of pieces (including *Mauser*, 1970) in which he challenges the contradictory reality of contemporary socialism, calling into question the extent of the sacrifice that the individual has to make under socialism. It was not until there was a change in official cultural policy in the course of the 1970s that he was able to establish himself properly, from which point on he was performed and published with increasing frequency in both East and West Berlin. His début abroad as one of the most important German dramatists since Brecht was substantiated in the early 1980s with a Heiner Müller festival in the Hague. In his latter-day work (which includes *Hamletmaschine*, 1977) Müller makes a more radical use of montage, producing fragmentary forms in an attempt to win back the subjective factor as an aesthetic category and to preserve the traces of subjectivity from the fossilizations of history. He thus epistemologically builds on the assumption that access to reality can only be fragmentary, that a disrupted relation to reality is the very principle from which to start.

The project of reclaiming the subjective factor from its repression does not, however, mean a new retreat into the private and personal. Subjectivity is rather to be seen as an eminently significant factor in politics. For now that forms of socialism have indeed been established there is always the danger that in confining the subject to the purely collective it will be driven into new forms of the reactionary and the regressive. The subjective element can no longer be ignored by a socialist state: the historical necessity of obtaining the subject's consent (*Einverständnis* in Brecht's sense) clashes with the desire of the individual for emancipation, where the full realization of socialism is uncertain or impossible. Müller wants to bring back the subject as part of the dialectic between the individual and history, to use it as an objective factor in political development and get away from the private irrational (which overshadowed Brecht's not dissimilar project in *Baal* and *Jungle*). He would want to go further than Pina Bausch in not only finding forms by means of which subjective levels of everyday experience can be traced and held, but also in showing their historical significance, though without reducing such experience to a particular historical plight, such as the effects of capitalism. What Müller does is to apply the dialectics of the past (Brecht's time) to the dialectics of the present (Müller's own time), a process which is aptly summarized by Girshausen:

> Brecht wrote for the self-recognition and change of capitalist society; Müller had to write for the self-recognition and change of socialist society, an uncertain, difficult society with few stable foundations, a society that – given its experiences with fascism and war – was scarcely attainable with naive optimism, and not attainable at all with revolutionary romanticism. (1981, p. 407)

Müller's position regarding Brecht has by no means been consistent, except in as much as Brecht has clearly been a force he has continually wanted to reckon with. In 1977 he declared his paramount interest in Brecht to be in the early work, the fragmentary pieces – especially *Fatzer*, and the *Lehrstücke* (see Müller, 1986, pp. 54 and 25). In 1977 Müller categorically rejected the *Lehrstück* as Brecht conceived it, writing to Reiner Steinweg that he thought it was best abandoned 'until the next earthquake' (in Steinweg (ed.), 1978, p. 232). In 1986, he argues that the conflict in *Mauser*, the play that tropes Brecht's *The Measures Taken*, has to be seen in a context of absolute extremity, that is to say, of the critical moments of past revolution. Whereas then it had been necessary to be economical with emotion, now there is again scope to deal with the emotions, in fact a need for 'an education of the emotions' (Müller, 1986, p. 191). Contrasting *Mauser* with *Hamletmaschine* will make plain what this difference involves.

Whatever his qualified reservations, Müller is one of the few dramatists in the GDR who engages productively and critically with the 'heritage' of the *Lehrstück*. Conceived as a theatre of participants only it points in the right direction for him, in that it presupposes art as a social practice, a co-operative labour which must gradually erode the distinction between producers and consumers, and challenge, if not change traditional notions of theatre. For him the very difficulty of texts is conducive of such a process, for it is precisely the experience with strange material which is thought-provoking (as distinct from mind-boggling), as long as such material does not raise false hopes by being presented as if it ought to be understood: 'having an experience surely resides in having something that cannot be immediately conceptualized' (Müller, 1986, p. 119). Hence it is not hard to see how from the formal point of view alone, not to speak of the content, any use of a *Fabel* would defeat this end.

Intervention on Brecht: Mauser

Mauser (1970) is the third of a trilogy of experimental pieces, the other two being *Philoktet* (1958–64) and *Der Horatier* (1968), in which the author explores with the use of material as diverse as myth, history, revolutionary struggle, the unacceptable face of revolution, and the excessive force required to maintain it. With *Mauser* Müller opens up the radical question of the meaning of sacrifice: he is not afraid to reveal the violence of individual experience as the subject is caught up in the historical process.

Mauser is a kind of deconstruction of Brecht's *The Measures Taken*. Brecht's play debates the problem of the individual *within* a collective, not that of the individual *versus* the collective, as is so often argued.[8] The Young Comrade, who jeopardizes the success of the revolution, is a member of the chorus and steps forward to act out his part retrospectively (a pattern that Müller retains with his protagonist B). For Brecht there can be no form of pure individualism while human beings are reduced to commodities: 'If the coolies are cheaper than rice, I can take a new coolie' is the trader's response to the plight of the coolies as they pull a rice boat up the river (*GW* 2, p. 649). What is required is identification with an oppressed class, rather than with a single member of that class. That is the substance of the *Fabel*; what the *Fabel* leaves out is the problem of the subject confronted with individual extinction, whether that of another or its own. Where Brecht's play had focused on the need for the emergence of a new kind of subject from the collective, one conscious of its role in bringing about the necessary transformation of history, even at the price of its own extinction, Müller focuses on the cost of that sacrifice and on the catastrophe of death as a real and final event, not merely a symbolic event that furthers the 'life' of the revolution. The 'consent' of the individual to his own death is more ambiguous in Müller's play, suggesting a new level of contradiction, where death might be regarded as an outcome of a philosophy of excessive force inseparable from any revolutionary enterprise. It is this problematic which is at the centre of the play *Mauser*, named after the pistol that transforms the man who uses it to kill.

Like Brecht's *The Measures Taken*, *Mauser* takes the form of a trial, seen partly in retrospect, has a chorus and functionaries rather than characters, and 'events' that are telescoped – the text consisting of barely fourteen pages of rhymeless verse with fugue-like repetitions of key-motifs. A is a professional executioner of the revolution, who has to kill his predecessor B because he allowed compassion to interfere with his duties. B makes a brief retrospective appearance to speak for his cause: 'Why the killing and why the dying/When the price of the revolution is the revolutionary/The price of freedom those to be freed' (Müller, 1978a, p. 59). Now A is prone to certain doubts of a rather different nature: he fears he is turning into a killing-machine. But the tribunal will not allow him to give up his office, maintaining that nothing human can thrive 'until the revolution has triumphed finally' (p. 63). This most Brechtian position is precisely what is being challenged, as will be seen. As A continues with his task he finds that instead of killing mechanically he loses himself in an orgy of killing, by his own account shooting 'again and again/Through the bursting skin into the bloody/Flesh and the splintering bones', the chorus commenting that 'he did not stop screaming/ With the voice of the human who devours the human/Then we knew that his work had consumed him' (pp. 64–5). He is thus not able to follow the doctrine of the party, namely that the 'work' of killing was 'bloody and like no other/But it must be done like other work/By someone or other' (p. 65). Because this failure denotes a lack of consciousness of what the revolutionary task entails, the party orders him to be shot as one of the 'enemies of the revolution' (p. 68), and he dies, himself joining in the call for the death of these enemies. His attitude, unlike that of the Young Comrade's in Brecht, is left ambiguous. To assess where he really situates himself, whether refusing or consenting, is a problem of defining one's position, a task for the audience.

Whereas for Brecht's Young Comrade learning consists in seeing the consequences of his betrayal of the revolution, A has insight into the process of revolution which leads to the betrayal of the people who are fighting it. In Müller's play the dialectical tension is between the revolutionary claim and the individual's inhumanity which is the result of the collectivized work of killing. Thus it is no longer a question of maintaining that the human can only come about as the end product of the revolution. Müller puts aside the death of the innocent Young Comrade and concentrates instead on the implicated party fighter who has killed in the wrong ways: either by killing like an automaton or like someone going berserk in an orgy of killing. Neither of these ways are acceptable to the party since they represent a loss of revolutionary conscious-ness: 'Your work has consumed you/You must disappear from the face of the earth' (p. 66). This harsh verdict is prepared for from the beginning by a fugue-like repetition of the ends justifying the means, 'we must yet tear out the grass to keep it green' (pp. 55, 59–60, 65, 68), yet there is also a continuous awareness, staged via the changing consciousness of A, of the terroristic nature of the revolutionary position.

The aesthetic aspect of the drama lies in the externalizing of A's innermost consciousness, achieved by the apparent de-historicizing of the text via the absence of plot and character-development, and the presentation of the issue as timeless and circular, as a recur-ring problem of any revolutionary endeavour. Unlike Brecht, it is not Müller's brief to educate the audience with respect to a particular historical moment in order to teach the mode of behav-iour adequate to that moment. His concern is rather to alert the audience to the violence of individual experience by awakening a sense of the loss of their own subjectivity. To this end he deliberately provokes a sense of shock. In the note appended to *Mauser*, Müller justifies an aesthetics of violence by maintaining that the use of the extreme case does not serve as an object in itself but as an example that is capable of bursting through the bounds of everyday normality. He thereby refuses the audience the comforts of sublimation as they are offered via the aesthetics of traditional comedy or tragedy. Instead of serving a transcendental function, death is rather to be seen as a function of life, as a production that is collectively organized and, by the same token, conducive to organizing the collective:

SO THAT SOMETHING CAN COME SOMETHING MUST GO THE FIRST SHAPE OF HOPE IS FEAR THE FIRST REVELATION OF THE NEW IS TERROR. (pp. 68–9)

Yet Müller is not so much committed to the transformation of the world, Brecht's project, as to the mediation of a general historical understanding of the cyclical nature of revolutionary killing, of death as an organized form of work. He is providing material for use (*Gebrauchsmaterial*) in the spirit of Brecht, but without guiding the audience as to how it might be used. Nevertheless, the implications of the 'terror' are inescapable: the destruction of the body is something that compulsively returns.

Teaching the unteachable: Hamletmaschine

Hamletmaschine is about the revolt of the body when exposed to the threat of violence and destruction. But this revolt has gone beyond the stage of being communicable in rational forms of language. It is a text 'in which the writing subject disintegrates into a series of identities, which merge into one another: Shakespeare, Ophelia, Hamlet, father, mother, whore, son; rebels and rulers' (Schulz, 1980, p. 149). The play itself is brief, even briefer than *Mauser*, consisting of barely nine pages. The text produces a veritable phantasmagoria of images and provokes the question of what a piece like this has to do with the theatre as we know it. It is indeed difficult to perform, which pleases Müller, for it is his contention that it is the task of literature to put up resistance against the theatre: 'only if a text cannot be done to suit the theatre in its present state, is it likely to be productive for the theatre, and interesting' (Müller, 1986, p. 18).

It is the tension between visual image and language which is so stimulating and productive, but which calls for a new kind of staging. My aim here is to relate Müller to the performance tradition in which his later work is conceived, rather than examine the text of *Hamletmaschine* for its own sake, as a particular piece in his oeuvre of pieces. Müller has taken considerable interest in the performance aspect of contemporary theatre, in particular the work of Richard Foreman and Robert Wilson, as well as that of Jerzy Grotowski and Antonin Artaud, the father of them all. In 1984, Müller collaborated with Wilson in Part II of the giant production in Cologne of Wilson's 'the CIVIL WarS', providing some of the texts and selecting others from world literature.[9]

Wilson's work is grounded in painting, architecture, and dance, and he derives a vast variety of formal structures from combining these arts. He functions simultaneously as scriptwriter, director, stage designer, and actor, and brings about a radical change in the theatrical event, partly by the unprecedented length of his productions, which are anything up to twelve hours and are meant to be attended to sporadically, often throughout the night. The verbal elements are monologic rather than dialogic: he uses both professional and non-professional actors as filters for a-signifying collective utterances, in particular an autistic boy whom he found in the street and whom he took to live with him. The 'text' is often initially a collective effort by those taking part and continues to call for collective endeavour on the part of the audience: his theatre produces a constant interplay of visual, verbal, and auditory elements, which problematize the relation of image to language and challenge the onlookers to occupy subjectively whatever spaces are offered for their fantasies. Wilson prefers not to address the audience directly, maintaining that he cannot tolerate a 'fascist' theatre, one that relies overmuch on 'confrontation and absorption': 'I like a great deal of space and I want the spectator to have sufficient space to have his own thoughts and ideas, inner impressions that are analogous to the outer ones on the stage.'[10]

This is precisely what attracted Müller to Wilson's work after some earlier misgivings. What he admires and what intrigues him is Wilson's refusal to do the work of interpretation:

> There's a text and it's delivered, but it is not evaluated and not coloured and not interpreted. It's there. Similarly, there's an image and the image isn't interpreted either, it's just there.

129

Then there's a noise, and that's there too and is also not interpreted. I regard this as important. It's a democratic concept of
theatre. Interpretation is the work of the spectator and is not to
take place on the stage. The spectator must not be absolved
from this work. That's consumerism . . . capitalist theatre.
(Müller and Ortolani, 1985, p. 91)

Wilson and Müller joined forces over *Hamletmaschine* in the course
of 1986. Its first staging was in New York, its second in Hamburg;
there was a production in London in November 1987.[11] Since the
Hamburg production was televised and could hence be recorded
on video and, ironically, fixed, it is possible to discuss the piece
with reference to this televised performance. Some of the visual
effects, such as changes of focus from close-ups of single figures to
distanced shots of groups would be denied to the stage, but
obviously the stage has recourse to a variety of aesthetic effects
denied to the camera. The equivalence of sensuous effect is clearly
much greater when it comes to auditory phenomena. What is
striking about the performance in general, whether staged or
filmed, is the way a text barely nine sides long, consisting of five
brief scenes of varying length, is converted into a session lasting
well over two hours. The most noticeable feature of the production
is the rigid repetition of a sequence of movements from scene to
scene, whereby what starts out as random is turned into an
expected pattern, re-contextualized in each scene by Müller's
script. The repetition is given peculiar force by the device of re-
arranging the stage perspective for each scene: everything on the
stage is moved clockwise by ninety degrees. Figures of idealization,
of authority, of psychotic withdrawal, interact within this ritualized
frame.

What is most striking about seeing and hearing the text, instead
of reading it, is the theatricalization of the space via light and
sound, particularly sound. Whereas the dance theatre of Pina
Bausch was a constant decentring of whatever sights were going
on, so that one was always missing something, in Wilson's staging
of the text this unsettling effect is chronically intensified by a
continual decentring of sound. There is an incessant collage of
different noises – a repeated snapping sound, sporadic bangs, and
a repetitive little tune with chromatic leaps played on an off-key
piano – some of which are in a kind of syncopation with both the
lighting effects and the speech or lack of speech. The tune evokes
the failure of romantic enchantment, the noises the contingency of

non-human nature both outside and inside the subject. The mono-
tony of all these sounds produces the effect of intermittent lapses
and regainings of attention to them, which induces a general
disorienting effect, disruptive in a way that does not occur in
Brecht's theatre.

Brecht did not experiment with a-signifying material, for it was
not part of his project to prise the spectator away from reality, but
rather to get him/her to reorganize and transform it. What experimental theatre has done from Artaud onwards is to play with the
formation of subjective spaces in order to disrupt and invade the
symbolization that has taken place in language. The body can be
made to speak by '*emptying* the phonemes of their distinctive
function . . . or else one can semanticize the phoneme', leading to
a text of voice:

> The method leads first to an experience of the splitting of
> perception: listening to the voice-sound can mean the loss of
> listening to the voice speech, comprehension of meaning; and
> listening to the voice-speech can occur at the expense of under-
> standing sound. In the same manner the attention one gives to
> the voice diminishes the attention one gives to the visual. After
> this splitting up which recalls an anterior stage of the subject,
> the perception of the sound-image-speech will have to be reorgan-
> ized for each of the auditors/spectators, and certainly in the
> unique difference of each one, according to their singular rela-
> tion to audio-visual languages. (Finter, 1983, p. 512)

The phonemic distortions of language are a powerful and original
means of undermining the authority system. This clearly goes
further and is radically different from any V-effect that Brecht
employed: whereas Brecht worked to subvert the existing forms of
language, Müller subverts the very processes by which language
comes to mean. The theatre of Wilson and Müller can thereby
become the analyst of the spectator's relation to language.

However, purely formal techniques are not just an end in
themselves in *Hamletmaschine*, but, as in the case of Brecht, they
point to a political content. There is a strong thematic element running through *Hamletmaschine*, which does not derive its name from its
forerunner without some purpose, and I will now turn to considering the relation of these themes to their radical presentation.

Müller's Hamlet is the intellectual gone bankrupt, bereft of his
function as critic and prophet. In scene 1 he declares at the outset,
'I was Hamlet. I stood on the shore and I talked with the serf

BLABLA, the ruins of Europe behind me' (Müller, 1978a, p. 89). In scene 3 he wants to be a woman and be dressed up in Ophelia's clothes. And in scene 4 he no longer appears as Hamlet, but as 'Hamlet-player' (*Hamletdarsteller*, p. 93). Müller's Hamlet is filled with nausea. He would like to opt out of history in analogous fashion to Shakespeare's hero ('The time is out of joint. O cursed spite,/That ever I was born to set it right!').[12] His wish to withdraw from history tropes Hamlet's desire for incest, generalizing it into a larger gesture which marks a longing to escape to a timeless realm free from oppression. He stumps about, dressed like a Hell's Angel, now and again mechanically sagging at the knee, spoken by a polyphony of voices, some amplified, others not, producing a stereophonic effect. To be or not to be a machine, that is the question. On the one hand, the nausea of killing, 'I don't want to kill any more': on the other hand, the way out, becoming a machine (like A in *Mauser*), 'I want to be a machine. Arms to grab legs to walk on no pain no thoughts' (1978a, p. 96). Yet even to be in a position to consider these as alternatives is a betrayal, a failure of commitment, as the Hamlet-player knows: 'I am a privileged person My nausea/is a privilege' (*ibid.*) and he tears up a photograph of Heiner Müller, author of *Hamletmaschine*.

Hamlet's failure to become a revolutionary subject is contrasted with Ophelia's refusal to remain a pathetic victim of male oppression. Her revolutionary potential lies in the experience of oppression which defines the revolutionary subject in general and woman in particular. She therefore becomes representative of the forces of anarchism and revolt which arise out of this situation. Yet, paradoxically, she is rigidly confined to a wheelchair, herself machinic in her desire for vengeance, performing jerky robot-like movements, manically scratching her head; sometimes she is a distant inconspicuous presence, sometimes she is in full close-up – eyes staring, semi-toothless mouth gaping wide open, coarse grey hair giving off wisps of dust, a voice issuing from elsewhere proclaiming her new role as Electra, seeking vengeance: 'It is Electra who speaks. In the heart of darkness. Under the sun of torture. To the capitals of the world. In the name of the victims' (p. 97). Though she is finally to be swathed in bandages from head to foot, she is nevertheless adopting the revolutionary position as against Hamlet's counter-revolutionary one, in that she appears as a woman, emancipated from her oppression, full of hate. The distinctions between the two are never quite clear-cut, since both figures are spoken by others, as well as uttering themselves. Two languages emerge most distinctly: a declamatory stage language which is elocuted by representative figures on the stage and which never comes from Ophelia in the chair, and another spasmodic, gasping, stuttering language, an intermittent echo of the first, mocking and sub-verting its clear enunciation. In both languages, the articulate and the inchoate, Electra/Ophelia repudiates her self-slaughter, her female functions of bearing and nursing children, and her role as sex object, and proclaims her revolutionary commitment, taking up the stance of a terrorist: 'Down with the joy of submission. Long live hate and contempt and rebellion and death. When she walks through your bedrooms holding butcher's-knives, you will know the truth' (p. 97). These are the final words (except for stage directions, which are spoken aloud throughout), marking an ironic shift from Hamlet's initial BLABLA to Ophelia/Electra's refusal of BLABLA via a hate-filled silence.

The five scenes of this play – like a parody of the traditional five-act drama – are neatly divided by a striking interlude. Scene 3 is a film-intermezzo, entitled 'Scherzo', with the caption 'The University of the Dead'. It consists of a colourful tableau of the figures taking part (unnamed in the text), including Hamlet and Ophelia, and is filmed virtually as a still, with occasional negligible but noticeable movement. Since the scene is filmed in vivid colour and dominated by a voice singing to vigorous piano accompani-ment a sombre German Lied, it is in powerful contrast with the stark whites, greys, and blacks of the other sets, with their random sounds. The whole tableau is finally engulfed in a conflagration of swirling flame. The written text of this scene appears as a string of subtitles:

> The university of the dead. Whispering and muttering. From their gravestones (rostrums) the dead philosophers throw their books at Hamlet. Gallery (ballet) of the dead women. The woman hanging from the rope. The woman with her arteries cut open etc. Hamlet looks at them with the attitude of a visitor to a museum (theatre). (p. 92)

The formal effect of this scene is extraordinary, an image of the horrors of history glossed over by the idealization of its survivors; at one point the still group, keeping its precise position, turns for a brief moment into a band of gorillas, a failure of the social order, no longer buttressed by the culture that was.

The hallmark of this performance is that there is hardly ever total silence, because of the constant background of disconcerting noises. In the latter half of the play these include rhythmic screams and screeches (known as 'scream-songs' in the language of performance theatre), retchings, groans, sobs, whispers, and finally sudden fragments of a popular tune blaring out shockingly to disrupt the silence staged at the end. Shocking though this is, it also fulfils a certain parodic function, implicit from the beginning, particularly through the all-pervasive presence of three female figures, seated upright at a table, with insane expressions on their faces, one hand rhythmically scratching or madly plucking at their hair, the other stiffly laid on the table, all in perfectly synchronized movements.

Müller has remarked that 'if you don't come to grips with *Hamletmaschine* as a comedy, you won't make anything out of this play' (Müller, 1986, p. 115). Comic elements in *Hamletmaschine* might be discerned in the way Brechtian targets are taken up and parodied throughout, such as the direness of getting stuck in history. The indications are in the written text both through the polyphony of voices which deconstruct great bourgeois tragedy with all its appurtenances and in the ironic figuring of the great themes of yesteryear. A radical intertextuality takes the place of dialogue and opens a space for the comic. In this production one way in which the reification of history is parodied is via the three zombie-like women, latter day Three Witches with nothing to prophesy. They are more than mere representatives of the reification of the world of things, of bureaucracy and economy: the reification is internalized (unlike Brecht's external social *gestus*) and going on inside their heads. The three, heavily made-up, have an air of masquerading as something, all in unconscious agreement as to what it is. The contradictions implicit in their appearance and demeanour are not consciously spelt out via a *Fabel*. Where Brecht attacks in full consciousness, Müller undermines via the unconscious, in this case disturbing the spectator's self-image by the patent inner automatism of these crazed superego-figures, full of ineffectual severity, performing pointless tasks. The supposed awe and sublimity of them as majestic fury-figures are comically at odds with their inane scratchings. They are ambiguous representatives of things in the psyche which control us; the V-effect is at the level of the psyche. Instead of, like Brecht, rendering a set of articulate beliefs ridiculous, Müller exposes and invades the self-image of the spectator, who laughs with some difficulty.

Müller is pessimistic about history. He updates *Hamlet*, making it relevant for our time: to indulge in anguish is a luxury. Like

Brecht, Müller is an iconoclast, but he does more than attack the icons of the bourgeois world: he goes for the very structures of the bourgeois self. Brecht launched a fierce attack on the attitudes that were the outcome of a particular system: Müller does not merely pick up Brecht's dialectics, but tropes them. He gets to the very genesis of the self, not the economic contradictions, but the contradictions in the construction of the psyche (which engaged Brecht in his early plays). That is the shock-effect of *Hamletmaschine*.

Brecht was trying to reconceptualize the historical process at a public level; Müller is reconceptualizing it at a private one. The self is social, because the social comes to dwell within it, but the body is not the individual that results. Müller's polyphonic discourse demonstrates that the body is mere contingency of matter, material out of which the self is made. He shows gruesomely the mess that results when the self-making apparatus, the machine, goes wrong and all the non-epistemized elements of the body flood the system and fill the world with noise. It is a pessimistic demonstration, since Müller makes it clear that this process is not necessarily revolutionary: the nausea of his Hamlet-player shows that modes of reaction against the system are often forms of the system, in that certain forms of revolution are bourgeois in themselves. With Müller one gets elements of the real which produce random contingent catastrophes. In what way, then, is it political theatre?

Müller's polyphonic discourse opposes the rationality of the enlightenment, the utopia of the old revolutions, and the optimism of Marxist communism. He provides a theatre that plays out the 'true' time of the subject (its fears and fantasies) as against the 'false' time of history, including literary history with its privileging of great works as 'accomplices of power'. 'I cannot keep politics out of the question of postmodernism', he writes, for the prefix 'post' in itself signifies for him the dividing up of cultural history in such a way that it becomes a metaphor for the domination of elites and power; while there is oppression in the world the issue must be the revolution of the oppressed, and that includes 'other cultures' (Müller, 1979, p. 1). To call his theatre 'postmodern' would for him still be tantamount with being defined in accordance with the categories of traditional aesthetics. Nevertheless, if the postmodern is that which introduces a certain resistance into the culture industry, that feeling of disturbance, of shock, which both Lyotard (see pp. 95–6) and Müller regard as the prerequisite of any change, then Müller's radical 'experimentation' (Lyotard) in the wake of the performing arts fulfils the condition of political theatre, the rude awakening of the spectator to a more chaotic beginning to what is to be done. Where Brecht thought he was teaching the teachable, Müller teaches of the unteachable, getting the spectator to confront the uncompromising nature of contingency in history and the body.

Notes

1 See Servos and Weigelt, 1984, for a biography and extensive illustrated account in English of Bausch's work; see also Hanraths and Winkels (eds), 1984, for a German collection of essays on her work.

2 Bausch's theatricalization of childhood seems to illustrate Jean Baudrillard's general point that 'women, children, animals – we must not be afraid of assimilations – do not just have a subject-consciousness, they have a kind of objective ironic presentiment that the category into which they have been placed does not exist. Which allows them at any given moment to make use of a double strategy' (1987, pp. 97–8). Baudrillard goes on to define this double strategy as one whereby the child 'has the possibility of offering himself as object, protected, recognized, destined as a child to the pedagogical function; and at the same time he is fighting on equal terms. At some level the child knows that he is not a child, but the adult does not know that. That is the secret' (pp. 96–7). Pina Bausch's theatre makes a speciality of exploring the strategies and secrets of the child/adult.

3 See, for example, Schivelbusch, 1974; Fehervary, 1976; Bathryck and Huyssen, 1976; Case, 1983; Müller and Heinitz, 1984.

4 See Müller, 1980, pp. 134–5; see also 'Reject it, in order to possess it', Girshausen, 1981.

5 For two excellent full-length studies, see Schulz, 1980, and Wieghaus, 1984; for a clear account in English, see Teraoka, 1985.

6 For an extensive account of Müller's reception, see Silberman, 1980.

7 See Mangel and Wieghaus, 1982, on whom this brief account of Müller's political position has drawn.

8 For a most interesting argument about the latter case, which goes against the usual position of regarding the Young Comrade's acceptance of his fate as merely following the party line, see Schivelbusch, 1974, who sees both Brecht and Müller as writers of 'optimistic tragedies', because they record a moment of true humanity that has not yet arrived.

9 See Michael Merschmeier's account in *Theater Heute*, 3, 1984, pp. 22–6, and Robert Wilson's own comments interspersed in Merschmeier's article.

10 In an interview with Peter Friedl (*Theater 1981*, pp. 77–82) Wilson discusses the problem of finding a language which catches the emotional nuances only to be found between the lines. He relates how

in the course of his work he finds himself returning to an experience
he had in America during the 1960s. He met a psychiatrist who had
made over 300 films of women talking intently to their crying babies.
When the films were run off in slow motion – twenty-four takes per
second – something more was seen than a mother comforting a child.
The initial takes showed the mother throwing herself on to her child
and the child defending itself. Further takes showed a succession of
different attitudes in the mother, revealing the complexity of emotions
between mother and child. The mother, when shown the film, was
appalled and said that she loved her child and only wanted to comfort
it (pp. 79–80).

Wilson works with the assumption that no text or gesture can ever
express something completely or adequately. Hence he tries to create
the conditions whereby the audience is free to have reactions.

11 See Henning Rischbieter in *Theater Heute*, 12, 1986, pp. 2–5, for an
illustrated account of the production at the Thalia Theatre, Hamburg.
The London production took place at the Almeida Theatre, Islington,
London, 4 to 14 November 1987, in a translation by Carl Weber.
Unfortunately, it occurred too late to include in this chapter, but it
seemed to match the Hamburg production very closely. For newspaper
reviews, see Granlund (1987), Jackson (1987), and Ratcliffe (1987) in
the references.

12 This quotation (*Hamlet*, I, v, ll. 189–90) is not included in Müller's
text, though he inserts a number of quotations from *Hamlet* in
German, as well as some English fragments which echo Shakespeare.

Conclusion

Brecht's achievement in divesting art of the auratic element has been followed by a new theatre that takes up the V-effect as transformed and refunctioned by artists and writers such as Bausch, Wilson, and Müller. This new theatre renders the modernist theatre repetitious and inert. To go on with mimesis in the theatre, however self-reflexive and questioning, is indeed to submit to the culture industry. Whereas in the past bourgeois positions were sustained by attitudes that were contingently produced by history (as Brecht's plays show) we are now in a world where the media are so manipulative that deliberate role-management and cynical exploitation has become endemic; hence it becomes imperative to alert people to the degree of their entrapment. This cannot be done by merely staging the old Brecht, for the political myths of yesteryear are, as he taught us, the anachronisms of today.

So what is to be done? Artists and writers such as Bausch, Wilson, and Müller implicitly or explicitly deconstruct Brecht's distinction between illusion and reality. To cross the frontier between illusion and reality is precisely to invade the insecurity of our self-image. Brecht wanted to disturb our ideological illusions, but the illusions he undermined via his theory were at the level of false consciousness. He himself, it must be granted, had no time for the consideration of the effects of unconscious fantasies.[1] Yet in his early writings, as has been shown, the boundaries between true and false, conscious and unconscious, are not so clear as his theory wants them to be, pointing to a postmodern understanding of fantasy and illusion.

Bausch and Müller reveal illusion as a necessary element of the social self: grasping the reality of subjects and objects involves illusion. The come-back of illusion as a 'normal' concomitant of perception is the central contribution of the postmodernist theatre, opening the way for a politics of postmodernism. Fascism has given illusion a bad name; one of the lacunae produced by recent history is that we have allowed illusion to lapse, being fearful of its use. Lacan's reading of Freud (who was also keen to drive a wedge between illusion and reality) and Althusser's reading of Marx have reinstated illusion as a central element of self-formation. In addressing the social construction of the subject and recognizing the part played by illusion in that construction, post-modernists are calling upon radicals to realize how much of aesthetics there is in politics.

Postmodernist artists show not only that the big narratives (the grand illusions) are no longer any use, but also that illusion of a kind is still inescapable because reality is not graspable any other way. The images in Müller's *Hamletmaschine* parody the machinic aspect of role: the 'characters' go mad because of their dis-illusion. The unteachable that Müller teaches is that the only hope lies in having illusions that are replaceable, exchangeable, and adaptable. That is the hopeful note: the comic in his plays points to the urgent need for adaptable illusions. The inevitable deduction made from Brecht's theory is that illusion is not merely false consciousness but that the self is illusory through and through. The aura surrounding the secure self-concept is thus shattered by a multiplicity of shocks as the subject discovers that its individual needs are not met and cannot be fully met by the collective purpose.

The corollary to Brecht's 'classical' theory is that the art/life boundaries have been breached in a more radical way than ever before. Any aesthetic activity will be part of life itself, a political act involving actors that are audiences and audiences that are actors. To speak with Lyotard, whatever 'rules' for the next illu-sion there have to be, they can in part be discovered *after* the event – they 'will have been done' (1984, p. 81). The aim is, perhaps, to discover what has emerged, to enter a game in order to produce the rules in order to find out who the players are. Hence the task of refunctioning Brecht is already part of a Brechtian reading of postmodernism, turning it back from a consumer culture to a culture which can collect the marginal individual.

Note

1 See Pietzker (1983), who discusses Brecht's scant relation to psychoanalysis in an interesting and well documented article, in which

he finds that, although Brecht had noted Freud as a major cultural thinker, he took no interest in psychoanalysis as a thought-system or a therapy. However, Pietzker cites passages to show that Brecht had an intuitive grasp of unconscious phenomena at the level of observation, but that, not surprisingly, he had no time for unconscious production, preferring to put his faith in reason and conscious knowledge: 'As a cure for "psychic problems" he recommends political activity' (p. 313). Pietzker ends with a discussion of the relation between Brecht's unconscious fantasies, as Pietzker sees them, and his personal, artistic, and political life. He concludes that, though Brecht was unable to make any changes in his unconscious patterns of behaviour through his political involvement, these patterns nevertheless had an effect on his political judgement.

References

Brecht

Brecht, Bertolt (1964) *Brecht on Theatre*, ed. and tr. John Willett, London: Methuen; referred to as Willett, 1964.

Brecht, Bertolt (1965) *The Messingkauf Dialogues*, tr. John Willett, London: Methuen; referred to as Willett, 1965.

Brecht, Bertolt (1967) *Gesammelte Werke*, 20 vols, Frankfurt: Suhrkamp; referred to as *GW*.

Brecht, Bertolt (1969) *Baal. Der böse Baal der asoziale. Texte, Varianten, Materialen*, ed. Dieter Schmidt, Frankfurt: Suhrkamp; referred to as Schmidt, 1969.

Brecht, Bertolt (1970–) *Collected Plays*, ed. John Willett and Ralph Manheim, London: Methuen; referred to as *CP*.

Brecht, Bertolt (1974) *Arbeitsjournal 1938–55*, ed. Werner Hecht, 2 vols, I, Frankfurt: Suhrkamp; referred to as *AJ*.

General

Adorno, Theodor W. (1952) *Versuch über Wagner*, Frankfurt: Suhrkamp.

Adorno, Theodor W. (1967) *Prisms*, tr. Samuel and Shierry Weber, London: Neville Spearman.

Adorno, Theodor W. (1971) *Gesammelte Schriften*, 23 vols, XII, 504.

Adorno, Theodor W. (1973) *The Philosophy of Modern Music*, tr. Anne G. Mitchell and Wesley V. Blomster, New York: Seabury Press.

Adorno, Theodor W. (1975) 'Culture industry reconsidered', *New German Critique* 6: 12–19.

Adorno, Theodor W. (1980) 'On commitment', in Anderson, Perry *et al.* (eds) (1980) *Aesthetics and Politics*, London: Verso, 177–95.

Anderson, Perry *et al.* (eds) (1980) *Aesthetics and Politics*, London: Verso.

Ash, Timothy Garton (1983) 'The poet and the butcher', *Times Literary Supplement*, 9 December: 1364–6.

Barthes, Roland (1975) *S/Z*, tr. Richard Miller, London: Jonathan Cape.

141

References

Barthes, Roland (1978) *A Lover's Discourse*, tr. Richard Howard, New York: Hill & Wang.

Barthes, Roland (1986) *The Rustle of Language*, Oxford: Basil Blackwell.

Bartram, Graham and Waine, Anthony (eds) (1982) *Brecht in Perspective*, London and New York: Longman.

Bathryck, David and Huyssen, Andreas (1976) 'Producing revolution: Heiner Müller's *Mauser* as a Learning Play', *New German Critique* 8: 110–21.

Baudrillard, Jean (1987) 'Forget Baudrillard', in *Forget Foucault*, Semiotext(e), New York: Columbia University, 65–135.

Baumgart, Richard (1987) 'Mönch Brecht', *Theater Heute* 2: 20.

Becker, Peter von (1981) 'Wer hat das Recht am Brecht? Zum neuesten Streit ums Erbe des reichen B.B.', *Theater Heute* 3: 1–2.

Benjamin, Walter (1973) *Understanding Brecht*, London: New Left Books.

Benjamin, Walter (1982) *Illuminations*, tr. Harry Zahn, ed. Hannah Arendt, London: Fontana/Collins.

Berenberg-Gossler, Heinrich, Müller, Hans-Harald, and Stosch, Joachim (1974) 'Das Lehrstück. Rekonstruktion einer Theorie oder Fortsetzung eines Lernprozesses', in Dyck, Joachim *et al.*, *Brechtdiskussion*, Kronberg: Scriptor, 121–71.

Berlau, Ruth, Brecht, Bertolt, Hubalek, Klaus, Palitsch, Peter, and Rülike, Käthe (1952) *Theaterarbeit*, ed. Berliner Ensemble, Dresden: Dresdener Verlag.

Berman, Russell (1977) 'Lukács' critique of Bredel and Ottwalt: a political account of an aesthetic debate of 1931–2', *New German Critique* 10: 155–78.

Brooker, Peter (1988) *Bertolt Brecht: Dialectics, Poetry, Politics*, London: Croom Helm.

Brüggemann, Heinz (1973) *Literarische Technik und soziale Revolution*, Reinbek bei Hamburg: Rowohlt.

Buck-Morss, Susan (1977) *The Origin of Negative Dialectics: Theodor W. Adorno, Walter Benjamin, and the Frankfurt Institute*, Hassocks, Sussex: Harvester Press.

Bürger, Peter (1984) *Theory of the Avant-Garde*, Minneapolis: University of Minnesota.

Case, Sue-Ellen (1983) 'From Bertolt Brecht to Heiner Müller', *Performing Arts Journal* 19: 94–102.

Christy, Desmond (1986) 'The echt Brecht test', *Guardian*, 8 March.

Claas, Herbert (1977) *Die politische Asthetik Bertolt Brechts vom Baal zum Caesar*, Frankfurt: Suhrkamp.

Deleuze, Gilles and Guattari, Félix (1976) *Kafka. Für eine kleine Literatur*, tr. Burkhart Kroeber, Frankfurt: Suhrkamp.

Deleuze, Gilles and Guattari, Félix (1977) *Anti-Oedipus: Capitalism and Schizophrenia*, tr. Robert Hurley, Mark Seem, and Helen R. Lane, New York: Viking Press.

Deleuze, Gilles and Guattari, Félix (1983) 'Rhizome', in *On the Line*, tr. John Johnston, Semiotext(e), New York: Columbia University.

References

Dickson, Keith A. (1978) *Towards Utopia: A Study of Brecht*, Oxford: Clarendon Press.

Eagleton, Terry (1981) *Walter Benjamin, or, Towards a Revolutionary Criticism*, London: Verso.

Eagleton, Terry (1985) 'Capitalism, modernism and postmodernism', *New Left Review* 152: 60–73.

Esslin, Martin (1959) *Brecht. A Choice of Evils. A Critical Study of the Man, his Work and his Opinions*, London: Eyre & Spottiswoode.

Fehervary, Helen (1976) 'Enlightenment or entanglement: history and aesthetics in Bertolt Brecht and Heiner Müller' *New German Critique* 8: 80–109.

Féral, Josette (1982) 'Performance and theatricality: the subject demystified', tr. Terese Lyons, *Modern Drama* 25, 1: 170–81.

Finter, Helga (1983) 'Experimental theatre and semiology of theatre: the theatricalization of voice', tr. E. A. Walker and Kathryn Grardal, *Modern Drama* 26, 4: 501–17.

Foucault, Michel (1983) *This is not a Pipe*, Berkeley, Los Angeles, London: University of California Press.

Freud, Sigmund (1953) *The Standard Edition of the Complete Psychological Works*, 24 vols, tr. James Strachey, London: Hogarth Press.

—— (1905) *Jokes and their Relation to the Unconscious*, VIII.

—— (1908) 'Creative writers and day-dreaming', IX, 141–53.

Fuegi, John (1987) *Bertolt Brecht: Chaos, According to Plan*, Cambridge: Cambridge University Press.

Gallas, Helga (1972) *Marxistische Literaturtheorie: Kontroversen im Bund proletarisch-revolutionärer Schriftsteller*, Neuwied and Berlin: Luchterhand.

Giese, Peter Christian (1974) *Das 'Gesellschaftlich-Komische': Zu Komik und Komödie am Beispiel der Stücke und Bearbeitungen Brechts*, Stuttgart: Metzler.

Girshausen, Theo (1981) '"Reject it, in order to possess it": On Heiner Müller and Bertolt Brecht', *Modern Drama* 23, 4: 404–21.

Granlund, Christopher (1987) 'Pinball ruins', Review of *Hamletmaschine*, *Guardian*, 23 October, 18.

Gray, Ronald (1976) *Brecht the Dramatist*, Cambridge: Cambridge University Press.

Guattari, Félix (1984) *Molecular Revolution: Psychiatry and Politics*, tr. Rosemary Sheed, Harmondsworth: Penguin.

Habermas, Jürgen (1970) 'Towards a theory of communicative competence', *Inquiry* 13: 360–75.

Habermas, Jürgen (1979) 'Consciousness-raising or redemptive criticism – the contemporary of Walter Benjamin', *New German Critique* 17: 30–59.

Habermas, Jürgen (1985a) 'Modernity – an incomplete project', in Hal Foster (ed.) *Postmodern Culture*, London and Sydney: Pluto Press, 3–15.

Habermas, Jürgen (1985b) 'Questions and counterquestions', in Richard J. Bernstein (ed.) *Habermas and Modernity*, Cambridge: Polity Press.

Habermas, Jürgen (1985c) *Die neue Unübersichtlichkeit: Kleine politische Schriften*, Frankfurt: Suhrkamp.

Handke, Peter (1968) 'Strassentheater und Theatertheater', *Theater Heute* 4: 6–7.

References

Hanraths, Ulrike and Winkels, Hubert (eds) (1984) *Tanzlegenden: Essays zu Pina Bausch's Tanztheater*, Frankfurt: Tende.

Haug, Fritz, Pierwoss, Klaus, and Ruoff, Karen (1980) *Aktualisierung Brechts*, Berlin: Argument Verlag.

Heath, Stephen (1974) 'Lessons from Brecht', *Screen*, Special Number: *Brecht and a Revolutionary Cinema*, 15, 2: 103–28.

Hegel, G.W.F. (1975) *Aesthetics: Lectures on Fine Art*, tr. T. M. Knox, 2 vols, Oxford: Oxford University Press.

Heise, Wolfgang (1964) 'Hegel und das Komische', *Sinn und Form: Beiträge zur Literatur* 16, 6: 811–30.

Hermand, Jost (1977) 'Brecht: Herr Puntila and sein Knecht Matti', in Hinck, Walter (ed.) (1977) *Die deutsche Komödie: Vom Mittelalter bis zur Gegenwart*, Düsseldorf: August Bagel Verlag, 287–304.

Hinderer, Walter (ed.) (1984) *Brecht's Dramen: Neue Interpretationen*, Stuttgart: Reclam.

Hofmann, Jürgen (1980) 'Die aufgeklärten Illusionsdramatiker gegen Brecht: Frisch, Grass, Handke', in Fritz Haug, Klaus Pierwoss, and Karen Ruoff (eds) *Aktualisierung Brechts*, Berlin: Argument Verlag, 143–53.

Horkheimer, Max and Adorno, Theodor W. (1973) *Dialectic of Enlightenment*, tr. John Cumming, London: Allen Lane.

Hutcheon, Linda (1988) *A Poetics of Postmodernism: History, Theory, Fiction*, London: Routledge.

Huyssen, Andreas (1975) 'Introduction to Adorno', *New German Critique* 6: 3–11.

Huyssen, Andreas (1983) 'Adorno in reverse: from Hollywood to Richard Wagner', *New German Critique* 29: 8–38.

Huyssen, Andreas (1984) 'Mapping the postmodern', *New German Critique* 33: 36–52.

Jackson, Kevin (1987) 'Listen with your eyes', interview with Robert Wilson, *Independent*, 31 October: 9.

Jameson, Fredric (1974) *Marxism and Form: Twentieth-Century Dialectical Theories of Literature*, Princeton, New Jersey: Princeton University Press.

Jameson, Fredric (1984) 'The politics of theory: ideological positions in the postmodernism debate', *New German Critique* 33: 53–65.

Jameson, Fredric (1985) 'Postmodernism and consumer society', in Hal Foster (ed.) *Postmodern Culture*, London: Pluto Press, 111–25.

Jay, Martin (1984) *Adorno*, London: Fontana.

Kamath, Rekha (1983) *Brechts Lehrstück als Bruch mit den bürgerlichen Theatertraditionen*, Frankfurt/Bern: Peter Lang.

Knopf, Jan (1974) *Bertolt Brecht. Ein Forschungsbericht. Fragwürdiges in der Brechtforschung*, Frankfurt: Fischer.

Knopf, Jan (1980) *Brecht-Hanbuch. Theater. Eine Asthetik der Widersprüche*, Stuttgart: Metzler.

Knopf, Jan (1984) *Brecht-Handbuch. Lyrik, Epik, Schriften. Eine Asthetik der Widersprüche*, Stuttgart: Metzler.

Lacan, Jacques (1977a) *Ecrits. A Selection*, tr. Alan Sheridan, London: Tavistock Publications.

References

Lacan, Jacques (1977b) *The Four Fundamental Concepts of Psycho-Analysis*, tr. Alan Sheridan, London: Hogarth Press.

Lehmann, Hans-Thies and Lethen, Helmut (1978) 'Ein Vorschlag zur Güte. Zur doppelten Polarität der Lehrstücke', in Reiner Steinweg (ed.) *Auf Anregung Bertolt Brechts: Lehrstücke mit Schülern, Arbeitern, Theaterleuten*, Frankfurt: Suhrkamp, 302–18.

Lichtheim, George (1970) *Lukács*, London: Fontana/Collins.

Lukács, Georg (1963) *The Meaning of Contemporary Realism*, London: Merlin Press.

Lukács, Georg (1969) 'Reportage oder Gestaltung', in Fritz Raddatz (ed.) *Marxismus und Literatur: Eine Dokumentation in drei Bänden*, II, Reinbek bei Hamburg: Rowohlt.

Lukács, Georg (1970) 'Narrate or describe?' in Arthur Kahn (ed. and tr.) *Writer and Critic*, London: Merlin Press, 110–48.

Lukács, Georg (1971) *History and Class Consciousness: Studies in Marxist Dialectics*, Cambridge, Massachusetts: MIT Press.

Lunn, Eugene (1985) *Marxism and Modernism: An Historical Study of Lukács, Brecht, Benjamin, and Adorno*, London: Verso.

Lyon, James K. (1982) *Bertolt Brecht in America*, London: Methuen.

Lyotard, Jean-François (1984) *The Postmodern Condition: A Report on Knowledge*, tr. Geoff Bennington and Brian Massumi, Minneapolis: University of Minnesota.

Lyotard, Jean-François (1986) 'Defining the postmodern', in Lisa Appignanesi (ed.) *Postmodernism. ICA Documents 4*, London: Institute of Contemporary Arts, 6–7.

Lyotard, Jean-François and Thébaud, Jean-Loup (1985) *Just Gaming*, tr. Wlad Godzich, Minneapolis: University of Minnesota.

McLeod, Ian (1980) 'Brecht and Sartre: problems of the committed playwright', unpublished PhD thesis, University of Oxford.

Mangel, Rüdiger and Wieghaus, Georg (1982) 'Abgrenzung und Teilhabe: Thesen zu Heiner Müllers Position im Literaturprozess der DDR', *Text und Kritik* 73: 32–44.

Marcuse, Herbert (1955) *Eros and Civilization*, London: Sphere Books.

Marx, Karl (1975 edn) 'Critique of Hegel's Philosophy of Right. Introduction', in *Early Writings*, tr. Rodney Livingstone and Gregor Benton, Harmondsworth: Penguin Books, 243–57.

Merschmeier, Michael (1984) 'Menschen, Tiere, Sensationen, Robert Wilsons "the CIVIL WarS": des Monsterprojekts zweite Etappe im Schauspiel Köln', *Theater Heute* 3: 22–6.

Mittenzwei, Werner (1977) *Wer war Brecht*, Berlin: Aufbau Verlag.

Müller, Heiner (1978a) *Mauser*, in *Mauser*, Berlin: Rotbuch Verlag, 55–69.

Müller, Heiner (1978b) *Hamletmaschine*, in *Mauser*, Berlin: Rotbuch Verlag, 89–97.

Müller, Heiner (1979) 'Der Schrecken, die erste Erscheinung des Neuen: Zu einer Diskussion über Postmodernismus in New York', *Theater Heute* 20: 1.

Müller, Heiner (1980) 'Brecht zu gebrauchen, ohne ihn zu kritisieren, ist

References

Verrat', *Theater 1980*, Jahrbuch von *Theater Heute*, 134–5.

Müller, Heiner (1981) 'Blut im Schuh oder das Rätsel der Freiheit', *Theater 1981*, Jahrbuch von *Theater Heute*, 34–5.

Müller, Heiner (1986) *Gesammelte Irrtümer: Interviews und Gespräche*, Frankfurt: Verlag der Autoren.

Müller, Heiner and Heinitz, Werner (1984) 'Das Vaterbild ist das Verhängnis', *Theater Heute* 1: 61–2.

Müller, Heiner and Ortolani, Olivier (1985) 'Die Form entsteht aus dem Maskieren', *Theater 1985*, Jahrbuch von *Theater Heute*, 88–91.

Nägele, Rainer (1987) *Reading after Freud: Essays on Goethe, Hölderlin, Habermas, Nietzsche, Brecht, Celan, and Freud*, New York: Columbia University Press.

Needle, Jan and Thomson, Peter (1981) *Brecht*, Oxford: Basil Blackwell.

Pachter, H. (1980) 'Brecht's personal politics', *Telos* (Summer) 44: 35–48.

Pavis, Patrice (1986) 'The classical heritage of modern drama: the case of postmodern theatre', tr. Loren Kruger, *Modern Drama* 29, 1: 1–22.

Pietzker, Carl (1983) 'Brecht's Verhältnis zur Psychoanalyse', *Amsterdamer Beiträge zur neueren Germanistik* 17: 275–317.

Poggioli, Renato (1968) *The Theory of the Avant-Garde*, Cambridge, Massachusetts: MIT Press.

Pontbriand, Chantal (1982) '"The eye finds no fixed point on which to rest. . ."', tr. C. R. Parsons, *Modern Drama* 25, 1: 154–62.

Ratcliffe, Michael (1987) 'Machinations: *Hamletmaschine* at the Almeida', *Observer*, 4 October.

Rischbieter, Henning (1986) 'Deutschland, Ein Wilsonmärchen: Über die Hamburger "Hamletmaschine"', *Theater Heute* 12: 2–7.

Russell, Charles (1985) *Poets, Prophets, and Revolutionaries: The Literary Avant-garde from Rimbaud through Postmodernism*, Oxford: Oxford University Press.

Schivelbusch, Wolfgang (1974) 'Optimistic tragedies: the plays of Heiner Müller', tr. Helen Fehervary, *New German Critique* 2: 104–13.

Schneider, Michael (1979) 'Bertolt Brecht – Ein abgebrochener Riese. Zur ästhetischen Emanzipation von einem Klassiker', *Literaturmagazin 10: Vorbilder*, Reinbek bei Hamburg: Rowohlt, 25–66.

Schulz, Genia (1980) *Heiner Müller*, Stuttgart: Metzler.

Servos, Norbert (1981) 'The emancipation of dance: Pina Bausch and the Wuppertal Dance Theatre', tr. Peter Harris and Pia Kleber, *Modern Drama* 22, 4: 435–47.

Servos, Norbert and Weigelt, Gert (1984) *Pina Bausch – Wuppertal Dance Theatre, or The Art of Training a Goldfish: Excursions into Dance*, Cologne: Ballet-Bühnen-Verlag.

Silberman, Marc (1980) *Heiner Müller*, Amsterdam: Rodopi.

Solomon, Maynard (ed.) (1979) *Marxism and Art: Essays Classic and Contemporary*, Brighton: Harvester Press.

Speirs, Ronald (1982) *Brecht's Early Plays*, London: Macmillan.

Steinweg, Reiner (1972a) *Das Lehrstück. Brechts Theorie einer ästhetischen Erziehung*, Stuttgart: Metzler.

References

Steinweg, Reiner (ed.) (1972b) *Bertolt Brecht: Die Massnahme, Kritische Ausgabe mit einer Spielanleitung von Reiner Steinweg*, Frankfurt: Suhrkamp.

Steinweg, Reiner (ed.) (1976) *Brechts Modell der Lehrstücke. Zeugnisse, Diskussionen, Erfahrungen*, Frankfurt: Suhrkamp.

Steinweg, Reiner (ed.) (1978) *Auf Anregung Bertolt Brechts: Lehrstücke mit Schülern, Arbeitern, Theaterleuten*, Frankfurt: Suhrkamp.

Suleiman, Susan Rubin (1984) 'Boston Shakespeare's new theatricality', review of *Mother Courage and her Children* (directed by Timothy Mayer) *Boston Review*, April, 16–17.

Suvin, Darko (1984) *To Brecht and Beyond: Soundings in Modern Dramaturgy*, Brighton: Harvester Press.

Szondi, Peter (1987) *Theory of the Modern Drama*, ed. and tr. Michael Hays, Cambridge: Polity Press.

Teraoka, Arlene Akiko (1985) *The Silence of Entropy or Universal Discourse: The Postmodernist Poetics of Heiner Müller*, New York, Berne, Frankfurt: Peter Lang.

Unseld, Siegfried (1980) *The Author and his Publisher*, tr. Hunter Hannum and Hildegard Hannum, Chicago: University of Chicago Press.

Voigts, Manfred (1977) *Brechts Theaterkonzeptionen. Entstehung und Entfaltung bis 1931*, Munich: Fink.

Wekwerth, Manfred (1980) 'Brecht-Theater in der Gegenwart', in Fritz Haug, Klaus Pierwoss, and Karen Ruoff (eds) *Aktualisierung Brechts*, Berlin: Argument Verlag, 101–22.

Wieghaus, Georg (1984) *Zwischen Auftrag und Verrat: Werk und Ästhetik Heiner Müllers*, Frankfurt: Peter Lang.

Willett, John (1959) *The Theatre of Bertolt Brecht*, London: Methuen.

Wilson, Robert and Friedl, Peter (1981) 'Die Balance zwischen den Wachträumen der Zuschauer und meinen eigenen Bildern zu finden', *Theater 1981*, Jahrbuch von *Theater Heute*, 77–82.

Wirth, Andrzej (1980) 'Vom Dialog zum Diskurs: Versuch einer Synthese der nachbrechtschen Theaterkonzepte', *Theater Heute* 1: 16–19.

Wright, Elizabeth (1984) *Psychoanalytic Criticism: Theory in Practice*, London: Methuen.

Wright, Elizabeth (1987) 'Transmission in psychoanalysis and literature: whose text is it anyway?' in Shlomith Rimmon-Kenan (ed.) *Discourse, Psychoanalysis and Literature*, London and New York: Methuen, 90–103.

Wyss, Monika (1977) *Brecht in der Kritik*, Munich: Kindler.

147

Index